The Power of Self Care/Self Love:
A Journal Workbook Into Your Higher Self

Jackie Castro-Cooper, MPT

The Power of Self Care/Self Love: A Journal Workbook Into Your Higher Self

©Copyright 2021 Jackie Castro-Cooper. All rights reserved.

ISBN: 978-1-954693-45-6

Thank you to Ms. Melz for the creation of the beautiful mandalas and for the wonderful cover from designer Michael Ilaqua.

No part of this book may be reproduced in any form, or by any means, or placed in storage retrieval systems without the express written permission of the publisher, except for newspaper, magazine, or other reviewers who wish to quote brief passages in reviews. Please respect Author's Rights.

Intellect Publishing, LLC
6581 County Road 32; Suite 1195
Point Clear, Alabama 36564 USA
www.IntellectPublishing.com

First Edition

Important note: Readers are strongly cautioned and advised to consult with a physician or other licensed health care professional before utilizing any of the information in this book. Neither the author nor publisher will be held liable.
FV – 17P
www.SelfCareSelfLoveBook.com

NOTE: Unattributed Quotes are by the Author.

Guest House by Rumi

This being human is a guest house.
Every morning a new arrival.

A joy, a depression, a meanness,
some momentary awareness comes
As an unexpected visitor.

Welcome and entertain them all!
Even if they're a crowd of sorrows,
who violently sweep your house
empty of its furniture,
still treat each guest honorably.
He may be clearing you out
for some new delight.

The dark thought, the shame, the malice,
meet them at the door laughing,
and invite them in.

Be grateful for whoever comes,
because each has been sent
as a guide from beyond.

The Power of Self Care/Self Love: A Journal Workbook Into Your Higher Self

The Power of Self Care/Self Love: A Journal Workbook Into Your Higher Self

Contents

The Guest House	p.3
Introduction	p.7-8
I am Affirmations	p.9
A Joy to Look Forward to	p.11-12
Choices for the Four Rooms	p.13-16
Ways to Prepare For Sleep	p.17-18
365 days of discoveries	p.21-386
Blank pages	p. 387-396

The Power of Self Care/Self Love: A Journal Workbook Into Your Higher Self

Beautiful Journal Friend,

The Power of Self Care/Self Love Journal Workbook you hold in your hand is a loving portal to your inner wisdom and a gateway to the next stanza of your life. Welcome to the Self Care/Self Love Movement!

I've had countless amazing journals in my life. The key to all of my evolutions has been in the pouring of my thoughts and feelings into those pages. Something magical happens when we write down our conversations with ourselves/God/universe. I believe it's connecting deeply with our subconscious, that part that controls 95% of what actually is going to manifest in our lives.

Why create a journal? After my book was published, *The Power of Self Care Self Love: A Physical Therapist's Guide to Evolving Into Your Higher Self,* I realized my readers could put the ideas from the book into practice if I created a simple companion journal. If you haven't read the book, you can still benefit tremendously from this journal since it can stand on its own.

For me personally, journal scribing has been a guide into my next stanza. The conversations have been between God/Intuition and myself, which I no longer feel as separate. Each journal has been my impetus forward into each evolution of my life. This journal is special because it awakens your true self...your higher self.

Whenever you start this journal it's the perfect time. Think of it as a new friend you've made in kindergarten. Hold its hand and explore your new exciting world together.

Each day starts off with a quote and exploratory questions where you can free flow your thoughts on paper. In those questions there is a transformative habit that changed my life based on a proverb. The proverb is, "You are a house with four rooms: The physical, intellectual, emotional, and spiritual rooms". Every day, you can choose to do something physical, learn something, feel an emotion, and connect with your inner wisdom/God/Universe/Spirit. Practicing this everyday allows the habit to be formed and a transformation to occur.

I've included lists to help in answering the exploratory questions. There are affirmations on those days that you wake up with no clue what to affirm, and a list of joys when joy is difficult to find. There are also suggestions of how to be physical, intellectual, emotional, and spiritual. And, there are recommendations to help you have a better night's sleep (check with your doctor first).

Around every 7 days you can, "Rest On a Quote". There's a whole page dedicated to exploring your inner wisdom. The number 7 holds the vibration of the intellect, ideas, and higher wisdom.

About every 15 days you'll explore, "What Do You Need?" This question has been pivotal for me throughout my many evolutions. The number 15 symbolizes new beginnings in love, success in love, major life changes, new choices, new ideas and new creative endeavors.

Almost every 40 days there will be a beautiful mandala you can color in if you choose to. Mandalas are a sacred space that can aid in meditation. The number 40 symbolizes the death of oneself and the spiritual rebirth. It is found in the Bible, the Koran, and the Torah.

Nearly every 90 days you'll have the choice of creating a vision board. The number 90 or 90 degrees indicates a balance between the forces of the spirit and the matter. Why a vision board? Because it's fun and you can physically create what your intuition is guiding you to manifest.

There are four vision boards, #1 What I Am Dreaming of Creating, #2 Places I Would Love to Visit, #3 What I Want to Start, #4 What I Am Grateful For.

The last 10 pages are blank to be used to write on, make a drawing, scotch tape a magazine cut out, or you can pull them out and collect them in a separate folder to use for your vision boards.

I encourage you to keep your journal near you. When inspiration strikes, you want to capture it here, like a butterfly net catching that brief encounter with your creative, honest, fun, divine thoughts.

This journal is the safe keeper and explorer of your evolutionary metamorphosis. Write freely and pour your heart out each day because you are the greatest gift to this world.

You are evolving, sweet friend. Enjoy the ride for the next 365 days!

With love and health (Con amor y salud),

Jackie Castro Cooper

P.S. If you have not read *The power of Self Care/Self Love: A Physical Therapist's Guide to Evolving Into Your Higher Self*, it will be a great companion book for you as you go deeper into your evolution.

I AM affirmations

Affirmations are a caring, loving way to bring us right back into our truth.

I am peace.
I am love.
I am pure love.
I am endless love.
I am grace.
I am divine.
I am the deep quiet.
I am this moment.
I am a gift.
I am powerful.
I am strong.
I am the universe.
I am powerful beyond measure.
I am connected to all living things.
I am beautiful.
I am all that is beautiful.
I am happy.
I am happiness.
I am good enough.
I am smart enough.
I am healing.
I am the universe.
I am choosing the path of least resistance.
I am a spiritual being having a human experience.
I am all that is good and loving in this world.

I am my higher self.
I am forgiveness.
I am laughter.
I am connected.
I am creative.
I am creating.
I am joy.
I am joy filled.
I am grateful.
I am in the present moment.
I am infinite.
I am that I am.
I am a work in progress.
I am ready.
I am a child of God.
I am truth.
I am the light.
I am healthy.
I am safe.
I am loved.
I am healing myself.

A Joy to look forward to

Experiencing joy reminds us that we are not here to suffer but to live.

Watching the sun rise.
Watching the sun set
Petting your cat.
Petting your dog.
Calling your friend.
Lying in a hammock.
Drinking coffee/tea in the morning.
Discovering a new coffee/tea shop.
Clean bed sheets.
A hot bath with music, essential oil, and candles.
Self-massage with coconut oil.
Reading a good book.
A yummy healthy breakfast.
Making a healthy tasty smoothie.
Watching a funny movie.
Having lunch with a friend.
Facetiming with someone special.
Saying I love you to yourself in the mirror.
Saying I love you to someone.
Hugging someone.
Enjoying a seasonal fruit.
Enjoying a seasonal vegetable.
Watching your favorite sports team.
Planning your next vacation.
Going on a vacation.
Buying yourself flowers.

Joy, cont'd.

Afternoon Tea.
Playing cards.
Taking a nap.
Playing a game.
Sitting at an outdoor cafe and watching people.
Going to a museum.
Buying someone a gift for no reason.
Happy hour with a friend.
Karaoke night.
Book club.
Movie night.
Going to a party.
Having a party.
Ice cream party.
Playing with a child.
Taking a painting class.
Taking a drawing class.
Taking a pottery class.
Listening to a beautiful song.

CHOICES FOR THE FOUR ROOMS

There is an Indian proverb: We are a house with four rooms, physical, intellectual, emotional, and spiritual. For a house to be livable and not become stale we must air out each room every day. *Active Self Time (AST) is moving your body and connecting with that part of your DNA that needs to be happy and active. Choose what the "self" is guiding you to do.

*PHYSICAL

Walk outdoors
Hike/Run
Yoga class
Kayak/canoe
Dance
Go to the gym
Lift weights
Do push ups
Bike ride
Zumba class
Jump/mini trampoline
Hula hoop
Create a garden
Swim
Pilates reformer
Walk on sand
Do QiGong
Do Tai Chi
Walk over a bridge
Snow skiing
Water skiing
Visit a farmer's market
Walk a Botanical Garden
Visit the zoo
Paint your kitchen
Sweep your floors
Walk/run intervals
Volunteer at a soup kitchen

Go camping

INTELLECTUAL

Read what you love
Listen to a podcast
Learn something new
Take a class
Join a book club
Go to a bookstore
Attend a lunch & learn
Write a book
Read a fun magazine
Listen to a Ted Talk
Draw something
Spend time with an elder
Spend time with a young person
Learn to play an instrument
Listen to classical music
Learn how your heart beats
Visit an aquarium
Build a computer
Build a table
Complete a crossword puzzle
Learn Sudoku
Start a new hobby
Study a religious book
Play a new game
Take a pottery class
Learn a new language
Write in this journal
Investigate your ancestry
Research the year you were born

EMOTIONAL

Have a good cry
Scream into a pillow
Watch a funny movie
Take a nap
Do Myofascial release
See a talk therapist
Talk to a trusted friend
Write a poem
Write a song
Get a massage
Listen to music and sing along
Do an abdominal massage
Play an instrument
Hold someone's hand
Touch someone's face
Hug yourself
Caress your own face
Massage your pet
Go fishing
Smile for 10 seconds
Make a new friend
Dance alone
Take a bubble bath
Write a letter to yourself
Write a letter to someone
Take yourself on a date
Use essential oil
Pare down your closet
Donate unloved items
Volunteer
Have a game night with friends

SPIRITUAL

Sit in silence
Meditate
Pray
Participate in a church community
Watch the rain
Take 10 deep breaths
Hug someone for 6 seconds
Listen to Gregorian Chant music
Sit in a temple/church/mosque
Sit by a body of water
Gaze at a mountain
Stare at a full moon
Watch the sun rise
Watch the sun set
Gaze into someone's eyes
Have lunch with a friend
Play with your pet
Do some gardening
Visit a greenhouse
Look closely at one flower
Do a sound healing class
Embrace a tree
Sing in a choir
Take a yoga class
Do a Buddhist meditation walk
Join a drum circle
Listen to singing bowls
Walk barefoot in the grass
Buy a homeless person lunch
Take a forest bath
Feel the sun on your skin
Gaze into someone's eyes
Have lunch with a friend
Sit in a temple/church/mosque
Sit by a body of water
Take 10 deep breaths
Hug someone for 6 seconds
Listen to Gregorian Chant music

WAYS TO PREPARE FOR SLEEP

Benefits of sleep: Good for your heart, decreases stress and inflammation, helps with memory and decision making, repairs cell damage, improves balance, promotes alertness, and may help in weight loss.

Dim the lights one hour before bedtime.

Remove all (or most) electronic devices from the bedroom.

Read an inspirational book in bed.

Take a warm bath.

Do a face massage. https://goop.com/wellness/health/face-massage-your-way-to-sleep/

Massage feet with coconut/almond/olive oil.

Do some Yoga stretches/twists before sleep.

Listen to a sleep Meditation.

Use an App for sleep: Insight timer, Headspace, or Calm.

Write down what you're worried about and leave it by your bed face down.

Write 5 or more things about the day that you're grateful for.

Use one or two ear plugs (When you sleep on your side you can use one).

Have a cup of hot chamomile tea.

Get a wake-up light alarm.

Try a cool mist dehumidifier or an essential oil diffuser.

WAYS TO PREPARE FOR SLEEP (cont'd)

Use lavender spray on pillows and in the bedroom (but not around pets).

Listen to 45 minutes of relaxing music (stimulates the parasympathetic nervous system so you can rest and digest) before sleep.

Try a white noise machine with recorded nature sounds or a simple sound like a fan.

Breathe in Lavender essential oil. Rub a drop into your palm. Rub hands together, cup your hands over your nose and breathe in three times.

The Power of Self Care/Self Love:
A Journal Workbook Into Your Higher Self

The Power of Self Care/Self Love: A Journal Workbook Into Your Higher Self

Journal writing gives us insights into who we are, who we were, and who we can become. -Sandra Marinella

Today is ___/___/___

In this moment I feel_____

I affirm that I am_____
(Choices of affirmations are on p. 9)

Where can I create joy today?_____
(Choices of joys are on p.11)

I am a House with Four Rooms. I will open and air out each room as a caring and loving gift for myself. (Choices for each are found on p. 13)

Physical_____

Intellectual_____

Emotional _____

Spiritual_____

🌙 Evening time pondering

What can I look forward to tomorrow?_____

5 things I am thankful for today_____

_____

_____

Sleep revitalizes me. I will prepare for sleep by_____
((Choices for preparation of sleep are on p. 17)

The Power of Self Care/Self Love: A Journal Workbook Into Your Higher Self

The place of indecision is a quiet place right before you sprout. It's uncomfortable but the potential will astound you.

Today is ___/___/___

In this moment I feel_____

I affirm that I am_____
(Choices of affirmations are on p. 9)

Where can I create joy today?_____
(Choices of joys are on p.11)

I am a House with Four Rooms. I will open and air out each room as a caring and loving gift for myself. (Choices for each are found on p. 13)

Physical_____

Intellectual_____

Emotional _____

Spiritual_____

☾ Evening time pondering

What can I look forward to tomorrow?_____

5 things I am thankful for today_____

_____

_____

Sleep revitalizes me. I will prepare for sleep by_____
((Choices for preparation of sleep are on p. 17)

The Power of Self Care/Self Love: A Journal Workbook Into Your Higher Self

The measure of Intelligence is the ability to change.
-Albert Einstein

Today is ___/___/___

In this moment I feel_____

I affirm that I am_____
(Choices of affirmations are on p. 9)

Where can I create joy today?_____
(Choices of joys are on p.11)

I am a House with Four Rooms. I will open and air out each room as a caring and loving gift for myself. (Choices for each are found on p. 13)

Physical_____

Intellectual_____

Emotional _____

Spiritual_____

🌙 Evening time pondering

What can I look forward to tomorrow?_____

5 things I am thankful for today_____

_____

_____

Sleep revitalizes me. I will prepare for sleep by_____
((Choices for preparation of sleep are on p. 17)

The Power of Self Care/Self Love: A Journal Workbook Into Your Higher Self

See yourself only through the loving eyes of God.

Today is ___/___/___

In this moment I feel_____

I affirm that I am_____
(Choices of affirmations are on p. 9)

Where can I create joy today?_____
(Choices of joys are on p.11)

I am a House with Four Rooms. I will open and air out each room as a caring and loving gift for myself. (Choices for each are found on p. 13)

Physical_____

Intellectual_____

Emotional _____

Spiritual_____

☽Evening time pondering

What can I look forward to tomorrow?_____

5 things I am thankful for today_____

_____

_____

Sleep revitalizes me. I will prepare for sleep by_____
((Choices for preparation of sleep are on p. 17)

The Power of Self Care/Self Love: A Journal Workbook Into Your Higher Self

If the only prayer you said was thank you, that would be enough.
-Meister Eckhart

Today is ___/___/___

In this moment I feel_____

I affirm that I am_____
(Choices of affirmations are on p. 9)

Where can I create joy today?_____
(Choices of joys are on p.11)

I am a House with Four Rooms. I will open and air out each room as a caring and loving gift for myself. (Choices for each are found on p. 13)

Physical_____

Intellectual_____

Emotional _____

Spiritual_____

🌙Evening time pondering

What can I look forward to tomorrow?_____

5 things I am thankful for today_____
_____
_____

Sleep revitalizes me. I will prepare for sleep by_____
((Choices for preparation of sleep are on p. 17)

The Power of Self Care/Self Love: A Journal Workbook Into Your Higher Self

I will love the light for it shows me the way. Yet, I will endure the darkness because it shows me the stars. -Eskimo Proverb

Today is ___/___/___

In this moment I feel_____

I affirm that I am_____
(Choices of affirmations are on p. 9)

Where can I create joy today?_____
(Choices of joys are on p.11)

I am a House with Four Rooms. I will open and air out each room as a caring and loving gift for myself. (Choices for each are found on p. 13)

Physical_____

Intellectual_____

Emotional _____

Spiritual_____

🌙Evening time pondering

What can I look forward to tomorrow?_____

5 things I am thankful for today_____

_____

_____

Sleep revitalizes me. I will prepare for sleep by_____
((Choices for preparation of sleep are on p. 17)

Dream. Do. Detach. - Robbi Mack

What are you dreaming about? What steps can you take to make it happen? Can you let go of the outcome?

_____

_____

_____

_____

_____

_____

_____

_____

_____

_____

_____

The Power of Self Care/Self Love: A Journal Workbook Into Your Higher Self

Seize the moment. Remember all those women on the Titanic who waved off the dessert cart. -Erma Bombeck

Today is ___/___/___

In this moment I feel_____

I affirm that I am_____
(Choices of affirmations are on p. 9)

Where can I create joy today?_____
(Choices of joys are on p.11)

I am a House with Four Rooms. I will open and air out each room as a caring and loving gift for myself. (Choices for each are found on p. 13)

Physical_____

Intellectual_____

Emotional _____

Spiritual_____

🌙 Evening time pondering

What can I look forward to tomorrow?_____

5 things I am thankful for today_____

_____

_____

Sleep revitalizes me. I will prepare for sleep by_____
((Choices for preparation of sleep are on p. 17)

The Power of Self Care/Self Love: A Journal Workbook Into Your Higher Self

Allow all that you create to be infused with love.

Today is ___/___/___

In this moment I feel_____

I affirm that I am_____
(Choices of affirmations are on p. 9)

Where can I create joy today?_____
(Choices of joys are on p.11)

I am a House with Four Rooms. I will open and air out each room as a caring and loving gift for myself. (Choices for each are found on p. 13)

Physical_____

Intellectual_____

Emotional _____

Spiritual_____

☾Evening time pondering

What can I look forward to tomorrow?_____

5 things I am thankful for today_____

_____

_____

Sleep revitalizes me. I will prepare for sleep by_____
((Choices for preparation of sleep are on p. 17)

The Power of Self Care/Self Love: A Journal Workbook Into Your Higher Self

Become the natural beauty that surrounds you.

Today is ___/___/___

In this moment I feel_____

I affirm that I am_____
(Choices of affirmations are on p. 9)

Where can I create joy today? _____
(Choices of joys are on p.11)

I am a House with Four Rooms. I will open and air out each room as a caring and loving gift for myself. (Choices for each are found on p. 13)

Physical_____

Intellectual_____

Emotional _____

Spiritual_____

☾Evening time pondering

What can I look forward to tomorrow?_____

5 things I am thankful for today_____

_____

_____

Sleep revitalizes me. I will prepare for sleep by_____
((Choices for preparation of sleep are on p. 17)

The Power of Self Care/Self Love: A Journal Workbook Into Your Higher Self

With God, all things are possible. -Book of Matthew

Today is ___/___/___

In this moment I feel_____

I affirm that I am_____
(Choices of affirmations are on p. 9)

Where can I create joy today? _____
(Choices of joys are on p.11)

I am a House with Four Rooms. I will open and air out each room as a caring and loving gift for myself. (Choices for each are found on p. 13)

Physical_____

Intellectual_____

Emotional _____

Spiritual_____

🌙Evening time pondering

What can I look forward to tomorrow?_____

5 things I am thankful for today_____

_____

_____

Sleep revitalizes me. I will prepare for sleep by_____
((Choices for preparation of sleep are on p. 17)

The Power of Self Care/Self Love: A Journal Workbook Into Your Higher Self

Fight for the things that you care about. But do it in a way that will lead others to join you. -Ruth Bader Ginsburg

Today is ___/___/___

In this moment I feel_____

I affirm that I am_____
(Choices of affirmations are on p. 9)

Where can I create joy today?_____
(Choices of joys are on p.11)

I am a House with Four Rooms. I will open and air out each room as a caring and loving gift for myself. (Choices for each are found on p. 13)

Physical_____

Intellectual_____

Emotional _____

Spiritual_____

🌙 Evening time pondering

What can I look forward to tomorrow?_____

5 things I am thankful for today_____
_____
_____

Sleep revitalizes me. I will prepare for sleep by_____
((Choices for preparation of sleep are on p. 17)

Give yourself permission to love yourself.

What would it be like if you loved yourself as much as you love your friend, partner, or your pet?

_____
_____
_____
_____
_____
_____
_____
_____
_____
_____
_____
_____
_____
_____

The Power of Self Care/Self Love: A Journal Workbook Into Your Higher Self

You are all that is good in this world.

Today is ___/___/___

In this moment I feel_____

I affirm that I am_____
(Choices of affirmations are on p. 9)

Where can I create joy today? _____
(Choices of joys are on p.11)

I am a House with Four Rooms. I will open and air out each room as a caring and loving gift for myself. (Choices for each are found on p. 13)

Physical_____

Intellectual_____

Emotional _____

Spiritual_____

☾Evening time pondering

What can I look forward to tomorrow?_____

5 things I am thankful for today_____

_____

_____

Sleep revitalizes me. I will prepare for sleep by_____
((Choices for preparation of sleep are on p. 17)

What Do You Need?

The Power of Self Care/Self Love: A Journal Workbook Into Your Higher Self

Connect with the Divine.

Today is ___/___/___

In this moment I feel_____

I affirm that I am_____
(Choices of affirmations are on p. 9)

Where can I create joy today? _____
(Choices of joys are on p.11)

I am a House with Four Rooms. I will open and air out each room as a caring and loving gift for myself. (Choices for each are found on p. 13)

Physical_____

Intellectual_____

Emotional _____

Spiritual_____

🌙Evening time pondering

What can I look forward to tomorrow?_____

5 things I am thankful for today_____

_____

_____

Sleep revitalizes me. I will prepare for sleep by_____
((Choices for preparation of sleep are on p. 17)

The Power of Self Care/Self Love: A Journal Workbook Into Your Higher Self

If you think that peace and happiness are somewhere else and you run after them, you will never arrive. -Thich Nhat Hanh

Today is ___/___/___

In this moment I feel_____

I affirm that I am_____
(Choices of affirmations are on p. 9)

Where can I create joy today? _____
(Choices of joys are on p.11)

I am a House with Four Rooms. I will open and air out each room as a caring and loving gift for myself. (Choices for each are found on p. 13)

Physical_____

Intellectual_____

Emotional _____

Spiritual_____

☽ Evening time pondering

What can I look forward to tomorrow?_____

5 things I am thankful for today_____

_____

_____

Sleep revitalizes me. I will prepare for sleep by_____
((Choices for preparation of sleep are on p. 17)

You should sit in meditation for 20 minutes a day, unless you're too busy. Then you should sit for an hour. -Zen Adage

Today is ___/___/___

In this moment I feel_____

I affirm that I am_____
(Choices of affirmations are on p. 9)

Where can I create joy today? _____
(Choices of joys are on p.11)

I am a House with Four Rooms. I will open and air out each room as a caring and loving gift for myself. (Choices for each are found on p. 13)

Physical_____

Intellectual_____

Emotional _____

Spiritual_____

☾Evening time pondering

What can I look forward to tomorrow?_____

5 things I am thankful for today_____

_____

_____

Sleep revitalizes me. I will prepare for sleep by_____
((Choices for preparation of sleep are on p. 17)

The Power of Self Care/Self Love: A Journal Workbook Into Your Higher Self

What you seek is already within you. -Dr. Harry Stafford

Today is ___/___/___

In this moment I feel_____

I affirm that I am_____
(Choices of affirmations are on p. 9)

Where can I create joy today? _____
(Choices of joys are on p.11)

I am a House with Four Rooms. I will open and air out each room as a caring and loving gift for myself. (Choices for each are found on p. 13)

Physical_____

Intellectual_____

Emotional _____

Spiritual_____

☾Evening time pondering

What can I look forward to tomorrow?_____

5 things I am thankful for today_____

_____

_____

Sleep revitalizes me. I will prepare for sleep by_____
((Choices for preparation of sleep are on p. 17)

Creativity is when we hold the hand of God/the Universe.

What would you like to create? Can you trust God/the Universe to guide you? Can you trust yourself?

_____

_____

_____

_____

_____

_____

_____

_____

_____

_____

_____

_____

_____

The Power of Self Care/Self Love: A Journal Workbook Into Your Higher Self

The struggle ends when the gratitude begins.
-Neale Donald Walsh

Today is ___/___/___

In this moment I feel_____

I affirm that I am_____
(Choices of affirmations are on p. 9)

Where can I create joy today? _____
(Choices of joys are on p.11)

I am a House with Four Rooms. I will open and air out each room as a caring and loving gift for myself. (Choices for each are found on p. 13)

Physical_____

Intellectual_____

Emotional _____

Spiritual_____

☽ Evening time pondering

What can I look forward to tomorrow?_____

5 things I am thankful for today_____

_____

_____

Sleep revitalizes me. I will prepare for sleep by_____
((Choices for preparation of sleep are on p. 17)

Night is always darker before dawn and life is the same. The hard times will pass, everything will get better, and the sun will shine brighter than ever. -Ernest Hemingway

Today is ___/___/___

In this moment I feel_____

I affirm that I am_____
(Choices of affirmations are on p. 9)

Where can I create joy today? _____
(Choices of joys are on p.11)

I am a House with Four Rooms. I will open and air out each room as a caring and loving gift for myself. (Choices for each are found on p. 13)

Physical_____

Intellectual_____

Emotional _____

Spiritual_____

☽Evening time pondering

What can I look forward to tomorrow?_____

5 things I am thankful for today_____

_____

_____

Sleep revitalizes me. I will prepare for sleep by_____
((Choices for preparation of sleep are on p. 17)

The Power of Self Care/Self Love: A Journal Workbook Into Your Higher Self

Trust in yourself.

Today is ___/___/___

In this moment I feel_____

I affirm that I am_____
(Choices of affirmations are on p. 9)

Where can I create joy today? _____
(Choices of joys are on p.11)

I am a House with Four Rooms. I will open and air out each room as a caring and loving gift for myself. (Choices for each are found on p. 13)

Physical_____

Intellectual_____

Emotional _____

Spiritual_____

☾Evening time pondering

What can I look forward to tomorrow?_____

5 things I am thankful for today_____

_____

_____

Sleep revitalizes me. I will prepare for sleep by_____
((Choices for preparation of sleep are on p. 17)

The Power of Self Care/Self Love: A Journal Workbook Into Your Higher Self

Take a risk today.

Today is ___/___/___

In this moment I feel_____

I affirm that I am_____
(Choices of affirmations are on p. 9)

Where can I create joy today? _____
(Choices of joys are on p.11)

I am a House with Four Rooms. I will open and air out each room as a caring and loving gift for myself. (Choices for each are found on p. 13)

Physical_____

Intellectual_____

Emotional _____

Spiritual_____

☾Evening time pondering

What can I look forward to tomorrow?_____

5 things I am thankful for today_____

_____

_____

Sleep revitalizes me. I will prepare for sleep by_____
((Choices for preparation of sleep are on p. 17)

The Power of Self Care/Self Love: A Journal Workbook Into Your Higher Self

You are being guided.

Today is ___/___/___

In this moment I feel_____

I affirm that I am_____
(Choices of affirmations are on p. 9)

Where can I create joy today? _____
(Choices of joys are on p.11)

I am a House with Four Rooms. I will open and air out each room as a caring and loving gift for myself. (Choices for each are found on p. 13)

Physical_____

Intellectual_____

Emotional _____

Spiritual_____

☾Evening time pondering

What can I look forward to tomorrow?_____

5 things I am thankful for today_____

_____

_____

Sleep revitalizes me. I will prepare for sleep by_____
((Choices for preparation of sleep are on p. 17)

The Power of Self Care/Self Love: A Journal Workbook Into Your Higher Self

Peace is a choice. -John Denver

Today is ___/___/___

In this moment I feel_____

I affirm that I am_____
(Choices of affirmations are on p. 9)

Where can I create joy today? _____
(Choices of joys are on p.11)

I am a House with Four Rooms. I will open and air out each room as a caring and loving gift for myself. (Choices for each are found on p. 13)

Physical_____

Intellectual_____

Emotional _____

Spiritual_____

☾Evening time pondering

What can I look forward to tomorrow?_____

5 things I am thankful for today_____

_____

_____

Sleep revitalizes me. I will prepare for sleep by_____
((Choices for preparation of sleep are on p. 17)

lead with love. -Lorrie Thomas Ross

What if today you see everyone, including yourself, through the eyes of love? What if the only words you speak today are loving words? Write below some things you love about yourself and your life.

The Power of Self Care/Self Love: A Journal Workbook Into Your Higher Self

Let go of the need to be right. -Dr. Wayne Dyer

Today is ___/___/___

In this moment I feel_____

I affirm that I am_____
(Choices of affirmations are on p. 9)

Where can I create joy today? _____
(Choices of joys are on p.11)

I am a House with Four Rooms. I will open and air out each room as a caring and loving gift for myself. (Choices for each are found on p. 13)

Physical_____

Intellectual_____

Emotional _____

Spiritual_____

☾Evening time pondering

What can I look forward to tomorrow?_____

5 things I am thankful for today_____

_____

_____

Sleep revitalizes me. I will prepare for sleep by_____
((Choices for preparation of sleep are on p. 17)

The Power of Self Care/Self Love: A Journal Workbook Into Your Higher Self

Joy comes from you who creates it. -Floralba Castro

Today is ___/___/___

In this moment I feel_____

I affirm that I am_____
(Choices of affirmations are on p. 9)

Where can I create joy today? _____
(Choices of joys are on p.11)

I am a House with Four Rooms. I will open and air out each room as a caring and loving gift for myself. (Choices for each are found on p. 13)

Physical_____

Intellectual_____

Emotional _____

Spiritual_____

☾Evening time pondering

What can I look forward to tomorrow?_____

5 things I am thankful for today_____
_____
_____

Sleep revitalizes me. I will prepare for sleep by_____
((Choices for preparation of sleep are on p. 17)

What Do You Need?

The Power of Self Care/Self Love: A Journal Workbook Into Your Higher Self

The word "spirit" comes from the Latin spiritus meaning a breath.

Today is ___/___/___

In this moment I feel_____

I affirm that I am_____
(Choices of affirmations are on p. 9)

Where can I create joy today? _____
(Choices of joys are on p.11)

I am a House with Four Rooms. I will open and air out each room as a caring and loving gift for myself. (Choices for each are found on p. 13)

Physical_____

Intellectual_____

Emotional _____

Spiritual_____

🌙 Evening time pondering

What can I look forward to tomorrow?_____

5 things I am thankful for today_____

_____

_____

Sleep revitalizes me. I will prepare for sleep by_____
((Choices for preparation of sleep are on p. 17)

The Power of Self Care/Self Love: A Journal Workbook Into Your Higher Self

Your heart and mind speak to each other.

Today is ___/___/___

In this moment I feel_____

I affirm that I am_____
(Choices of affirmations are on p. 9)

Where can I create joy today? _____
(Choices of joys are on p.11)

I am a House with Four Rooms. I will open and air out each room as a caring and loving gift for myself. (Choices for each are found on p. 13)

Physical_____

Intellectual_____

Emotional _____

Spiritual_____

☾Evening time pondering

What can I look forward to tomorrow?_____

5 things I am thankful for today_____

_____

_____

Sleep revitalizes me. I will prepare for sleep by_____
((Choices for preparation of sleep are on p. 17)

The Power of Self Care/Self Love: A Journal Workbook Into Your Higher Self

Be kind whenever possible. It's always possible. -Dalai Lama

Today is ___/___/___

In this moment I feel_____

I affirm that I am_____
(Choices of affirmations are on p. 9)

Where can I create joy today? _____
(Choices of joys are on p.11)

I am a House with Four Rooms. I will open and air out each room as a caring and loving gift for myself. (Choices for each are found on p. 13)

Physical_____

Intellectual_____

Emotional _____

Spiritual_____

🌙Evening time pondering

What can I look forward to tomorrow?_____

5 things I am thankful for today_____

_____

_____

Sleep revitalizes me. I will prepare for sleep by_____
((Choices for preparation of sleep are on p. 17)

You Are Divine

You are more than this body. There is a life force, a field that runs through you and the universe. What does this force feel like to you?

_____

_____

_____

_____

_____

_____

_____

_____

_____

_____

_____

_____

The Power of Self Care/Self Love: A Journal Workbook Into Your Higher Self

Your journey does not have to be hard.

Today is ___/___/___

In this moment I feel_____

I affirm that I am_____
(Choices of affirmations are on p. 9)

Where can I create joy today? _____
(Choices of joys are on p.11)

I am a House with Four Rooms. I will open and air out each room as a caring and loving gift for myself. (Choices for each are found on p. 13)

Physical_____

Intellectual_____

Emotional _____

Spiritual_____

☾Evening time pondering

What can I look forward to tomorrow?_____

5 things I am thankful for today_____

_____

_____

Sleep revitalizes me. I will prepare for sleep by_____
((Choices for preparation of sleep are on p. 17)

The Power of Self Care/Self Love: A Journal Workbook Into Your Higher Self

The body is a sacred garment. It is your first and last garment... and it should be treated with honor. -Martha Graham

Today is ___/___/___

In this moment I feel_____

I affirm that I am_____
(Choices of affirmations are on p. 9)

Where can I create joy today? _____
(Choices of joys are on p.11)

I am a House with Four Rooms. I will open and air out each room as a caring and loving gift for myself. (Choices for each are found on p. 13)

Physical_____

Intellectual_____

Emotional _____

Spiritual_____

☾Evening time pondering

What can I look forward to tomorrow?_____

5 things I am thankful for today_____

_____

_____

Sleep revitalizes me. I will prepare for sleep by_____
((Choices for preparation of sleep are on p. 17)

To forgive is to set a prisoner free and discover that prisoner was you. -Lewis B. Smedes

Today is ___/___/___

In this moment I feel_____

I affirm that I am_____
(Choices of affirmations are on p. 9)

Where can I create joy today? _____
(Choices of joys are on p.11)

I am a House with Four Rooms. I will open and air out each room as a caring and loving gift for myself. (Choices for each are found on p. 13)

Physical_____

Intellectual_____

Emotional _____

Spiritual_____

🌙Evening time pondering

What can I look forward to tomorrow?_____

5 things I am thankful for today_____

_____

_____

Sleep revitalizes me. I will prepare for sleep by_____
((Choices for preparation of sleep are on p. 17)

Laughter heals you.

Today is ___/___/___

In this moment I feel_____

I affirm that I am_____
(Choices of affirmations are on p. 9)

Where can I create joy today? _____
(Choices of joys are on p.11)

I am a House with Four Rooms. I will open and air out each room as a caring and loving gift for myself. (Choices for each are found on p. 13)

Physical_____

Intellectual_____

Emotional _____

Spiritual_____

🌙 Evening time pondering

What can I look forward to tomorrow?_____

5 things I am thankful for today_____

_____

_____

Sleep revitalizes me. I will prepare for sleep by_____
((Choices for preparation of sleep are on p. 17)

The Power of Self Care/Self Love: A Journal Workbook Into Your Higher Self

If there is to be any peace it will come from being, not having.
-Henry Miller

Today is ___/___/___

In this moment I feel_____

I affirm that I am_____
(Choices of affirmations are on p. 9)

Where can I create joy today? _____
(Choices of joys are on p.11)

I am a House with Four Rooms. I will open and air out each room as a caring and loving gift for myself. (Choices for each are found on p. 13)

Physical_____

Intellectual_____

Emotional _____

Spiritual_____

☾Evening time pondering

What can I look forward to tomorrow?_____

5 things I am thankful for today_____

_____

_____

Sleep revitalizes me. I will prepare for sleep by_____
((Choices for preparation of sleep are on p. 17)

Feel your negative emotions, and then let them go

Fear, anger, anxiety, sadness, grief, shame, guilt...need to be felt. The body senses them as false when they linger too long. What can you feel and let go of?

The Power of Self Care/Self Love: A Journal Workbook Into Your Higher Self

There is a loving light that is always around you.

Today is ___/___/___

In this moment I feel_____

I affirm that I am_____
(Choices of affirmations are on p. 9)

Where can I create joy today? _____
(Choices of joys are on p.11)

I am a House with Four Rooms. I will open and air out each room as a caring and loving gift for myself. (Choices for each are found on p. 13)

Physical_____

Intellectual_____

Emotional _____

Spiritual_____

🌙Evening time pondering

What can I look forward to tomorrow?_____

5 things I am thankful for today_____

_____

_____

Sleep revitalizes me. I will prepare for sleep by_____
((Choices for preparation of sleep are on p. 17)

The Power of Self Care/Self Love: A Journal Workbook Into Your Higher Self

Love is all you need. -Paul McCartney

Today is ___/___/___

In this moment I feel_____

I affirm that I am_____
(Choices of affirmations are on p. 9)

Where can I create joy today? _____
(Choices of joys are on p.11)

I am a House with Four Rooms. I will open and air out each room as a caring and loving gift for myself. (Choices for each are found on p. 13)

Physical_____

Intellectual_____

Emotional _____

Spiritual_____

☾Evening time pondering

What can I look forward to tomorrow?_____

5 things I am thankful for today_____

_____

_____

Sleep revitalizes me. I will prepare for sleep by_____
((Choices for preparation of sleep are on p. 17)

The Power of Self Care/Self Love: A Journal Workbook Into Your Higher Self

Tomorrow never comes. There is only today.
-(Mawelita) Carmen Maria Gallindo

Today is ___/___/___

In this moment I feel_____

I affirm that I am_____
(Choices of affirmations are on p. 9)

Where can I create joy today? _____
(Choices of joys are on p.11)

I am a House with Four Rooms. I will open and air out each room as a caring and loving gift for myself. (Choices for each are found on p. 13)

Physical_____

Intellectual_____

Emotional _____

Spiritual_____

☾Evening time pondering

What can I look forward to tomorrow?_____

5 things I am thankful for today_____

_____

_____

Sleep revitalizes me. I will prepare for sleep by_____
((Choices for preparation of sleep are on p. 17)

What Do You Need?

The Power of Self Care/Self Love: A Journal Workbook Into Your Higher Self

Take a good look at the sky.

Today is ___/___/___

In this moment I feel_____

I affirm that I am_____
(Choices of affirmations are on p. 9)

Where can I create joy today? _____
(Choices of joys are on p.11)

I am a House with Four Rooms. I will open and air out each room as a caring and loving gift for myself. (Choices for each are found on p. 13)

Physical_____

Intellectual_____

Emotional _____

Spiritual_____

☾Evening time pondering

What can I look forward to tomorrow?_____

5 things I am thankful for today_____

_____

_____

Sleep revitalizes me. I will prepare for sleep by_____
((Choices for preparation of sleep are on p. 17)

The Power of Self Care/Self Love: A Journal Workbook Into Your Higher Self

Feel the sun on your skin.

Today is ___/___/___

In this moment I feel_____

I affirm that I am_____
(Choices of affirmations are on p. 9)

Where can I create joy today? _____
(Choices of joys are on p.11)

I am a House with Four Rooms. I will open and air out each room as a caring and loving gift for myself. (Choices for each are found on p. 13)

Physical_____

Intellectual_____

Emotional _____

Spiritual_____

🌙 Evening time pondering

What can I look forward to tomorrow?_____

5 things I am thankful for today_____

_____

_____

Sleep revitalizes me. I will prepare for sleep by_____
((Choices for preparation of sleep are on p. 17)

67

***The only person you are destined to become is the person you decide to be.* -Ralph Waldo Emerson**

Who are you deciding to be? Being has nothing to do with your career or your position in your family.

_____

_____

_____

_____

_____

_____

_____

_____

_____

_____

_____

_____

The Power of Self Care/Self Love: A Journal Workbook Into Your Higher Self

The mirror reflects the soul.

Today is ___/___/___

In this moment I feel_____

I affirm that I am_____
(Choices of affirmations are on p. 9)

Where can I create joy today? _____
(Choices of joys are on p.11)

I am a House with Four Rooms. I will open and air out each room as a caring and loving gift for myself. (Choices for each are found on p. 13)

Physical_____

Intellectual_____

Emotional _____

Spiritual_____

🌙 Evening time pondering

What can I look forward to tomorrow?_____

5 things I am thankful for today_____

_____

_____

Sleep revitalizes me. I will prepare for sleep by_____
((Choices for preparation of sleep are on p. 17)

The Power of Self Care/Self Love: A Journal Workbook Into Your Higher Self

There is a world out there...go see it.

Today is ___/___/___

In this moment I feel_____

I affirm that I am_____
(Choices of affirmations are on p. 9)

Where can I create joy today? _____
(Choices of joys are on p.11)

I am a House with Four Rooms. I will open and air out each room as a caring and loving gift for myself. (Choices for each are found on p. 13)

Physical_____

Intellectual_____

Emotional _____

Spiritual_____

☾Evening time pondering

What can I look forward to tomorrow?_____

5 things I am thankful for today_____

_____

_____

Sleep revitalizes me. I will prepare for sleep by_____
((Choices for preparation of sleep are on p. 17)

The Power of Self Care/Self Love: A Journal Workbook Into Your Higher Self

As we accept that we are Divine, everything around us changes.

Today is ___/___/___

In this moment I feel_____

I affirm that I am_____
(Choices of affirmations are on p. 9)

Where can I create joy today? _____
(Choices of joys are on p.11)

I am a House with Four Rooms. I will open and air out each room as a caring and loving gift for myself. (Choices for each are found on p. 13)

Physical_____

Intellectual_____

Emotional _____

Spiritual_____

🌙Evening time pondering

What can I look forward to tomorrow?_____

5 things I am thankful for today_____

_____

_____

Sleep revitalizes me. I will prepare for sleep by_____
((Choices for preparation of sleep are on p. 17)

The Power of Self Care/Self Love: A Journal Workbook Into Your Higher Self

Inside myself is a place where I live all alone, and that's where you renew your springs that never dry up. -Pearl S. Buck

Today is ___/___/___

In this moment I feel_____

I affirm that I am_____
(Choices of affirmations are on p. 9)

Where can I create joy today? _____
(Choices of joys are on p.11)

I am a House with Four Rooms. I will open and air out each room as a caring and loving gift for myself. (Choices for each are found on p. 13)

Physical_____

Intellectual_____

Emotional _____

Spiritual_____

☾Evening time pondering

What can I look forward to tomorrow?_____

5 things I am thankful for today_____

_____

_____

Sleep revitalizes me. I will prepare for sleep by_____
((Choices for preparation of sleep are on p. 17)

The Power of Self Care/Self Love: A Journal Workbook Into Your Higher Self

Be aware of the brevity of life.

Today is ___/___/___

In this moment I feel_____

I affirm that I am_____
(Choices of affirmations are on p. 9)

Where can I create joy today? _____
(Choices of joys are on p.11)

I am a House with Four Rooms. I will open and air out each room as a caring and loving gift for myself. (Choices for each are found on p. 13)

Physical_____

Intellectual_____

Emotional _____

Spiritual_____

🌙 Evening time pondering

What can I look forward to tomorrow?_____

5 things I am thankful for today_____

_____

_____

Sleep revitalizes me. I will prepare for sleep by_____
((Choices for preparation of sleep are on p. 17)

The Power of Self Care/Self Love: A Journal Workbook Into Your Higher Self

Our creative dreams and yearnings come from a Divine source. As we move toward our dreams, we move toward our Divinity.
-Julia Cameron

Today is ___/___/___

In this moment I feel_____

I affirm that I am_____
(Choices of affirmations are on p. 9)

Where can I create joy today? _____
(Choices of joys are on p.11)

I am a House with Four Rooms. I will open and air out each room as a caring and loving gift for myself. (Choices for each are found on p. 13)

Physical_____

Intellectual_____

Emotional _____

Spiritual_____

☾Evening time pondering

What can I look forward to tomorrow?_____

5 things I am thankful for today_____

_____

_____

Sleep revitalizes me. I will prepare for sleep by_____
((Choices for preparation of sleep are on p. 17)

Doubt has no place here.

What would happen if you no longer doubted yourself?

_____
_____
_____
_____
_____
_____
_____
_____
_____
_____
_____
_____
_____
_____
_____

The Power of Self Care/Self Love: A Journal Workbook Into Your Higher Self

In life, winning and losing will both happen. What is never acceptable is quitting. -Magic Johnson

Today is ___/___/___

In this moment I feel_____

I affirm that I am_____
(Choices of affirmations are on p. 9)

Where can I create joy today? _____
(Choices of joys are on p.11)

I am a House with Four Rooms. I will open and air out each room as a caring and loving gift for myself. (Choices for each are found on p. 13)

Physical_____

Intellectual_____

Emotional _____

Spiritual_____

☾Evening time pondering

What can I look forward to tomorrow?_____

5 things I am thankful for today_____

_____

_____

Sleep revitalizes me. I will prepare for sleep by_____
((Choices for preparation of sleep are on p. 17)

The Power of Self Care/Self Love: A Journal Workbook Into Your Higher Self

Dive into your inner wisdom, the well of infinite love and creativity.

Today is ___/___/___

In this moment I feel_____

I affirm that I am_____
(Choices of affirmations are on p. 9)

Where can I create joy today? _____
(Choices of joys are on p.11)

I am a House with Four Rooms. I will open and air out each room as a caring and loving gift for myself. (Choices for each are found on p. 13)

Physical_____

Intellectual_____

Emotional_____

Spiritual_____

🌙 Evening time pondering

What can I look forward to tomorrow?_____

5 things I am thankful for today_____
_____
_____

Sleep revitalizes me. I will prepare for sleep by_____
((Choices for preparation of sleep are on p. 17)

The Power of Self Care/Self Love: A Journal Workbook Into Your Higher Self

You are your higher self.

Today is ___/___/___

In this moment I feel_____

I affirm that I am_____
(Choices of affirmations are on p. 9)

Where can I create joy today? _____
(Choices of joys are on p.11)

I am a House with Four Rooms. I will open and air out each room as a caring and loving gift for myself. (Choices for each are found on p. 13)

Physical_____

Intellectual_____

Emotional _____

Spiritual_____

☾Evening time pondering

What can I look forward to tomorrow?_____

5 things I am thankful for today_____

_____

_____

Sleep revitalizes me. I will prepare for sleep by_____
((Choices for preparation of sleep are on p. 17)

The Power of Self Care/Self Love: A Journal Workbook Into Your Higher Self

Your body, mind, and spirit are holy: Treat them as such.
–(Mawelita) Carmen Maria Gallindo

Today is ___/___/___

In this moment I feel_____

I affirm that I am_____
(Choices of affirmations are on p. 9)

Where can I create joy today? _____
(Choices of joys are on p.11)

I am a House with Four Rooms. I will open and air out each room as a caring and loving gift for myself. (Choices for each are found on p. 13)

Physical_____

Intellectual_____

Emotional _____

Spiritual_____

🌙Evening time pondering

What can I look forward to tomorrow?_____

5 things I am thankful for today_____

_____

_____

Sleep revitalizes me. I will prepare for sleep by_____
((Choices for preparation of sleep are on p. 17)

What Do You Need?

The Power of Self Care/Self Love: A Journal Workbook Into Your Higher Self

Hands to work, hearts to God. -Shaker Axiom

Today is ___/___/___

In this moment I feel_____

I affirm that I am_____
(Choices of affirmations are on p. 9)

Where can I create joy today? _____
(Choices of joys are on p.11)

I am a House with Four Rooms. I will open and air out each room as a caring and loving gift for myself. (Choices for each are found on p. 13)

Physical_____

Intellectual_____

Emotional _____

Spiritual_____

🌙Evening time pondering

What can I look forward to tomorrow?_____

5 things I am thankful for today_____
_____
_____

Sleep revitalizes me. I will prepare for sleep by_____
((Choices for preparation of sleep are on p. 17)

Connect with your evolutionary metamorphosis.

What changes are you feeling within you?
Are you evolving or staying in your comfort zone?

_____
_____
_____
_____
_____
_____
_____
_____
_____
_____
_____
_____
_____

The Power of Self Care/Self Love: A Journal Workbook Into Your Higher Self

When we connect or become one with the Divine higher vibrational frequencies, wonderful things begin to happen.

Today is ___/___/___

In this moment I feel_____

I affirm that I am_____
(Choices of affirmations are on p. 9)

Where can I create joy today? _____
(Choices of joys are on p.11)

I am a House with Four Rooms. I will open and air out each room as a caring and loving gift for myself. (Choices for each are found on p. 13)

Physical_____

Intellectual_____

Emotional _____

Spiritual_____

☾Evening time pondering

What can I look forward to tomorrow?_____

5 things I am thankful for today_____

_____

_____

Sleep revitalizes me. I will prepare for sleep by_____
((Choices for preparation of sleep are on p. 17)

Only by trying can you enrich yourself and have the possibility of moving forward. The greatest obstacle in life is fear and giving up because of it. -Justice Sonia Sotomayor

Today is ___/___/___

In this moment I feel_____

I affirm that I am_____
Choices of affirmations are on p. 6)

Where can I create joy today? _____
(Choices of joys are on p.11)

I am a House with Four Rooms. I will open and air out each room as a caring and loving gift for myself. (Choices for each are found on p. 13)

Physical_____

Intellectual_____

Emotional _____

Spiritual_____

☾Evening time pondering

What can I look forward to tomorrow?_____

5 things I am thankful for today_____

_____

_____

Sleep revitalizes me. I will prepare for sleep by_____
((Choices for preparation of sleep are on p. 17)

The Power of Self Care/Self Love: A Journal Workbook Into Your Higher Self

The practice of forgiveness is our most important contribution to the healing of the world. -Marianne Williamson

Today is ___/___/___

In this moment I feel_____

I affirm that I am_____
(Choices of affirmations are on p. 9)

Where can I create joy today? _____
(Choices of joys are on p.11)

I am a House with Four Rooms. I will open and air out each room as a caring and loving gift for myself. (Choices for each are found on p. 13)

Physical_____

Intellectual_____

Emotional _____

Spiritual_____

☾Evening time pondering

What can I look forward to tomorrow?_____

5 things I am thankful for today_____
_____
_____

Sleep revitalizes me. I will prepare for sleep by_____
((Choices for preparation of sleep are on p. 17)

The Power of Self Care/Self Love: A Journal Workbook Into Your Higher Self

Instead of building walls, we should be building bridges.
-Vicente Fox

Today is ___/___/___

In this moment I feel_____

I affirm that I am_____
(Choices of affirmations are on p. 9)

Where can I create joy today? _____
(Choices of joys are on p.11)

I am a House with Four Rooms. I will open and air out each room as a caring and loving gift for myself. (Choices for each are found on p. 13)

Physical_____

Intellectual_____

Emotional _____

Spiritual_____

☾Evening time pondering

What can I look forward to tomorrow?_____

5 things I am thankful for today_____

_____

_____

Sleep revitalizes me. I will prepare for sleep by_____
((Choices for preparation of sleep are on p. 17)

The Power of Self Care/Self Love: A Journal Workbook Into Your Higher Self

It's time to shift into your new paradigm.

Today is ___/___/___

In this moment I feel_____

I affirm that I am_____
(Choices of affirmations are on p. 9)

Where can I create joy today? _____
(Choices of joys are on p.11)

I am a House with Four Rooms. I will open and air out each room as a caring and loving gift for myself. (Choices for each are found on p. 13)

Physical_____

Intellectual_____

Emotional _____

Spiritual_____

☾Evening time pondering

What can I look forward to tomorrow?_____

5 things I am thankful for today_____

_____

_____

Sleep revitalizes me. I will prepare for sleep by_____
((Choices for preparation of sleep are on p. 17)

Dedicate the next 15 minutes to listening to yourself.

Write what you hear on this page.

Follow what you are genuinely passionate about and let that guide you to your destination. -Diane Sawyer

Today is ___/___/___

In this moment I feel_____

I affirm that I am_____
(Choices of affirmations are on p. 9)

Where can I create joy today? _____
(Choices of joys are on p.11)

I am a House with Four Rooms. I will open and air out each room as a caring and loving gift for myself. (Choices for each are found on p. 13)

Physical_____

Intellectual_____

Emotional _____

Spiritual_____

🌙 Evening time pondering

What can I look forward to tomorrow?_____

5 things I am thankful for today_____

_____

_____

Sleep revitalizes me. I will prepare for sleep by_____ (

The Power of Self Care/Self Love: A Journal Workbook Into Your Higher Self

Be the bearer of good news.

Today is ___/___/___

In this moment I feel_____

I affirm that I am_____
(Choices of affirmations are on p. 9)

Where can I create joy today? _____
(Choices of joys are on p.11)

I am a House with Four Rooms. I will open and air out each room as a caring and loving gift for myself. (Choices for each are found on p. 13)

Physical_____

Intellectual_____

Emotional _____

Spiritual_____

☾Evening time pondering

What can I look forward to tomorrow?_____

5 things I am thankful for today_____

_____

_____

Sleep revitalizes me. I will prepare for sleep by_____
((Choices for preparation of sleep are on p. 17)

The Power of Self Care/Self Love: A Journal Workbook Into Your Higher Self

What door do you need to open?

Today is ___/___/___

In this moment I feel_____

I affirm that I am_____
(Choices of affirmations are on p. 9)

Where can I create joy today? _____
(Choices of joys are on p.11)

I am a House with Four Rooms. I will open and air out each room as a caring and loving gift for myself. (Choices for each are found on p. 13)

Physical_____

Intellectual_____

Emotional _____

Spiritual_____

☾Evening time pondering

What can I look forward to tomorrow?_____

5 things I am thankful for today_____

_____

_____

Sleep revitalizes me. I will prepare for sleep by_____
((Choices for preparation of sleep are on p. 17)

The Power of Self Care/Self Love: A Journal Workbook Into Your Higher Self

Everything you need is already within you. -Brian Tracy

Today is ___/___/___

In this moment I feel_____

I affirm that I am_____
(Choices of affirmations are on p. 9)

Where can I create joy today? _____
(Choices of joys are on p.11)

I am a House with Four Rooms. I will open and air out each room as a caring and loving gift for myself. (Choices for each are found on p. 13)

Physical_____

Intellectual_____

Emotional _____

Spiritual_____

☽Evening time pondering

What can I look forward to tomorrow?_____

5 things I am thankful for today_____

_____

_____

Sleep revitalizes me. I will prepare for sleep by_____
((Choices for preparation of sleep are on p. 17)

Those who dare to fail miserably can achieve greatly.
-President John F. Kennedy

Today is ___/___/___

In this moment I feel_____

I affirm that I am_____
(Choices of affirmations are on p. 9)

Where can I create joy today? _____
(Choices of joys are on p.11)

I am a House with Four Rooms. I will open and air out each room as a caring and loving gift for myself. (Choices for each are found on p. 13)

Physical_____

Intellectual_____

Emotional _____

Spiritual_____

☽Evening time pondering

What can I look forward to tomorrow?_____

5 things I am thankful for today_____

_____

_____

Sleep revitalizes me. I will prepare for sleep by_____
((Choices for preparation of sleep are on p. 17)

The Power of Self Care/Self Love: A Journal Workbook Into Your Higher Self

Feel everything...then move forward.

Today is ___/___/___

In this moment I feel_____

I affirm that I am_____
(Choices of affirmations are on p. 9)

Where can I create joy today? _____
(Choices of joys are on p.11)

I am a House with Four Rooms. I will open and air out each room as a caring and loving gift for myself. (Choices for each are found on p. 13)

Physical_____

Intellectual_____

Emotional _____

Spiritual_____

🌙 Evening time pondering

What can I look forward to tomorrow?_____

5 things I am thankful for today_____

_____

_____

Sleep revitalizes me. I will prepare for sleep by_____
((Choices for preparation of sleep are on p. 17)

What Do You Need?

The Power of Self Care/Self Love: A Journal Workbook Into Your Higher Self

You are the gift.

Today is ___/___/___

In this moment I feel_____

I affirm that I am_____
(Choices of affirmations are on p. 9)

Where can I create joy today? _____
(Choices of joys are on p.11)

I am a House with Four Rooms. I will open and air out each room as a caring and loving gift for myself. (Choices for each are found on p. 13)

Physical_____

Intellectual_____

Emotional _____

Spiritual_____

🌙Evening time pondering

What can I look forward to tomorrow?_____

5 things I am thankful for today_____

_____

_____

Sleep revitalizes me. I will prepare for sleep by_____
((Choices for preparation of sleep are on p. 17)

With the new day comes new strengths and new thoughts. -Eleanor Roosevelt

What new thoughts are you having right now?

___

___

___

___

___

___

___

___

___

___

___

___

___

___

___

See the good in others.

Today is ___/___/___

In this moment I feel_____

I affirm that I am_____
(Choices of affirmations are on p. 9)

Where can I create joy today? _____
(Choices of joys are on p.11)

I am a House with Four Rooms. I will open and air out each room as a caring and loving gift for myself. (Choices for each are found on p. 13)

Physical_____

Intellectual_____

Emotional _____

Spiritual_____

🌙 Evening time pondering

What can I look forward to tomorrow?_____

5 things I am thankful for today_____

_____

_____

Sleep revitalizes me. I will prepare for sleep by_____
((Choices for preparation of sleep are on p. 17)

I would like to achieve a state of inner spiritual grace from which I could function and give as I was meant to in the eye of God.
-Anne Morrow Lindbergh

Today is ___/___/___

In this moment I feel_____

I affirm that I am_____
(Choices of affirmations are on p. 9)

Where can I create joy today? _____
(Choices of joys are on p.11)

I am a House with Four Rooms. I will open and air out each room as a caring and loving gift for myself. (Choices for each are found on p. 13)

Physical_____

Intellectual_____

Emotional _____

Spiritual_____

☽Evening time pondering

What can I look forward to tomorrow?_____

5 things I am thankful for today_____

_____

_____

Sleep revitalizes me. I will prepare for sleep by_____
((Choices for preparation of sleep are on p. 17)

The Power of Self Care/Self Love: A Journal Workbook Into Your Higher Self

The Power of Self Care/Self Love: A Journal Workbook Into Your Higher Self

Care for and love yourself first.

Today is ___/___/___

In this moment I feel_____

I affirm that I am_____
(Choices of affirmations are on p. 9)

Where can I create joy today? _____
(Choices of joys are on p.11)

I am a House with Four Rooms. I will open and air out each room as a caring and loving gift for myself. (Choices for each are found on p. 13)

Physical_____

Intellectual_____

Emotional _____

Spiritual_____

🌙 Evening time pondering

What can I look forward to tomorrow?_____

5 things I am thankful for today_____

_____

_____

Sleep revitalizes me. I will prepare for sleep by_____
((Choices for preparation of sleep are on p. 17)

The Power of Self Care/Self Love: A Journal Workbook Into Your Higher Self

Love is not only something you feel, it's something you do.
-David Wilkerson

Today is ___/___/___

In this moment I feel_____

I affirm that I am_____
(Choices of affirmations are on p. 9)

Where can I create joy today? _____
(Choices of joys are on p.11)

I am a House with Four Rooms. I will open and air out each room as a caring and loving gift for myself. (Choices for each are found on p. 13)

Physical_____

Intellectual_____

Emotional _____

Spiritual_____

☾Evening time pondering

What can I look forward to tomorrow?_____

5 things I am thankful for today_____

_____

_____

Sleep revitalizes me. I will prepare for sleep by_____
((Choices for preparation of sleep are on p. 17)

The Power of Self Care/Self Love: A Journal Workbook Into Your Higher Self

Today you can begin again.

Today is ___/___/___

In this moment I feel_____

I affirm that I am_____
(Choices of affirmations are on p. 9)

Where can I create joy today? _____
(Choices of joys are on p.11)

I am a House with Four Rooms. I will open and air out each room as a caring and loving gift for myself. (Choices for each are found on p. 13)

Physical_____

Intellectual_____

Emotional _____

Spiritual_____

☾Evening time pondering

What can I look forward to tomorrow?_____

5 things I am thankful for today_____

_____

_____

Sleep revitalizes me. I will prepare for sleep by_____
((Choices for preparation of sleep are on p. 17)

The more you practice gratitude, the more you see how much there is to be grateful for. -Don Miguel Ruiz

Your life's journey up to today has been filled with good things. What are they?

_____

_____

_____

_____

_____

_____

_____

_____

_____

_____

_____

_____

Open your hands to receive.

Today is ___/___/___

In this moment I feel_____

I affirm that I am_____
(Choices of affirmations are on p. 9)

Where can I create joy today? _____
(Choices of joys are on p.11)

I am a House with Four Rooms. I will open and air out each room as a caring and loving gift for myself. (Choices for each are found on p. 13)

Physical_____

Intellectual_____

Emotional _____

Spiritual_____

☾Evening time pondering

What can I look forward to tomorrow?_____

5 things I am thankful for today_____

_____

_____

Sleep revitalizes me. I will prepare for sleep by_____
((Choices for preparation of sleep are on p. 17)

The Power of Self Care/Self Love: A Journal Workbook Into Your Higher Self

There is endless love all around us.

Today is ___/___/___

In this moment I feel_____

I affirm that I am_____
(Choices of affirmations are on p. 9)

Where can I create joy today? _____
(Choices of joys are on p.11)

I am a House with Four Rooms. I will open and air out each room as a caring and loving gift for myself. (Choices for each are found on p. 13)

Physical_____

Intellectual_____

Emotional _____

Spiritual_____

🌙Evening time pondering

What can I look forward to tomorrow?_____

5 things I am thankful for today_____

_____

_____

Sleep revitalizes me. I will prepare for sleep by_____
((Choices for preparation of sleep are on p. 17)

The Power of Self Care/Self Love: A Journal Workbook Into Your Higher Self

Choose to step into the Light that is always around you.

Today is ___/___/___

In this moment I feel_____

I affirm that I am_____
(Choices of affirmations are on p. 9)

Where can I create joy today? _____
(Choices of joys are on p.11)

I am a House with Four Rooms. I will open and air out each room as a caring and loving gift for myself. (Choices for each are found on p. 13)

Physical_____

Intellectual_____

Emotional _____

Spiritual_____

☽Evening time pondering

What can I look forward to tomorrow?_____

5 things I am thankful for today_____

_____

_____

Sleep revitalizes me. I will prepare for sleep by_____
((Choices for preparation of sleep are on p. 17)

The Power of Self Care/Self Love: A Journal Workbook Into Your Higher Self

I was exhilarated by the realization that I could change...my life by changing my beliefs. I... realized that there was a science-based path that would take me from my job as a perennial "victim" to my new position as "co-creator" of my destiny. -Dr. Bruce H. Lipton

Today is ___/___/___

In this moment I feel_____

I affirm that I am_____
(Choices of affirmations are on p. 9)

Where can I create joy today? _____
(Choices of joys are on p.11)

I am a House with Four Rooms. I will open and air out each room as a caring and loving gift for myself. (Choices for each are found on p. 13)

Physical_____

Intellectual_____

Emotional _____

Spiritual_____

☾Evening time pondering

What can I look forward to tomorrow?_____

5 things I am thankful for today_____

_____

_____

Sleep revitalizes me. I will prepare for sleep by_____
((Choices for preparation of sleep are on p. 17)

The Power of Self Care/Self Love: A Journal Workbook Into Your Higher Self

Vision Board #1:
What I Am Dreaming of Creating

It's been 90 days and it's time to indulge yourself in a fun activity: your first vision board.

Why a vision board? For me, it brings to life what I am dreaming about. I can touch and see clearly, right before my eyes, what I would like to create. It is a powerful way to speak to my subconscious and manifest my dreams.

Like a scavenger hunt, look for what you have cut out or printed and taped to the last 10 pages. Is there anything there that represents what you want to create? If there is not much there then take some time today to explore magazines, newspapers, Pinterest, or Canva and cut out and print your items on an 11x14 (or larger) cork board, thick poster board, magnetic dry erase board, or canvas.

There are no rules, just a fun exploration of what your body, mind and spirit want to create.

Vision boards can have:
sticky notes
Colored paper sheets
3x5 index cards
A poem
Well-thought-out typed words
Pictures of what you love
Real pictures of you, family, friends

Remember, this is a fun activity so grab your scissors, glue, scotch tape, markers, push pins or magnets.

What Do You Need?

The Power of Self Care/Self Love: A Journal Workbook Into Your Higher Self

Your body wants to feel every loving thought.

Today is ___/___/___

In this moment I feel_____

I affirm that I am_____
(Choices of affirmations are on p. 9)

Where can I create joy today? _____
(Choices of joys are on p.11)

I am a House with Four Rooms. I will open and air out each room as a caring and loving gift for myself. (Choices for each are found on p. 13)

Physical_____

Intellectual_____

Emotional _____

Spiritual_____

🌙Evening time pondering

What can I look forward to tomorrow?_____

5 things I am thankful for today_____

_____

_____

Sleep revitalizes me. I will prepare for sleep by_____
((Choices for preparation of sleep are on p. 17)

If you believe it will work out, you'll see opportunities.
-Dr. Wayne Dyer

What do you need to believe in? Why?

_____

_____

_____

_____

_____

_____

_____

_____

_____

_____

_____

_____

The Power of Self Care/Self Love: A Journal Workbook Into Your Higher Self

There is wisdom within you.

Today is ___/___/___

In this moment I feel_____

I affirm that I am_____
(Choices of affirmations are on p. 9)

Where can I create joy today? _____
(Choices of joys are on p.11)

I am a House with Four Rooms. I will open and air out each room as a caring and loving gift for myself. (Choices for each are found on p. 13)

Physical_____

Intellectual_____

Emotional _____

Spiritual_____

☾Evening time pondering

What can I look forward to tomorrow?_____

5 things I am thankful for today_____

_____

_____

Sleep revitalizes me. I will prepare for sleep by_____
((Choices for preparation of sleep are on p. 17)

The Power of Self Care/Self Love: A Journal Workbook Into Your Higher Self

Be yourself, but always your better self. -Karl G. Maeser

Today is ___/___/___

In this moment I feel_____

I affirm that I am_____
(Choices of affirmations are on p. 9)

Where can I create joy today? _____
(Choices of joys are on p.11)

I am a House with Four Rooms. I will open and air out each room as a caring and loving gift for myself. (Choices for each are found on p. 13)

Physical_____

Intellectual_____

Emotional _____

Spiritual_____

🌙Evening time pondering

What can I look forward to tomorrow?_____

5 things I am thankful for today_____

_____

_____

Sleep revitalizes me. I will prepare for sleep by_____
((Choices for preparation of sleep are on p. 17)

The Power of Self Care/Self Love: A Journal Workbook Into Your Higher Self

The Divine lives within you. -Joseph Campbell

Today is ___/___/___

In this moment I feel_____

I affirm that I am_____
(Choices of affirmations are on p. 9)

Where can I create joy today? _____
(Choices of joys are on p.11)

I am a House with Four Rooms. I will open and air out each room as a caring and loving gift for myself. (Choices for each are found on p. 13)

Physical_____

Intellectual_____

Emotional _____

Spiritual_____

☾Evening time pondering

What can I look forward to tomorrow?_____

5 things I am thankful for today_____

_____

_____

Sleep revitalizes me. I will prepare for sleep by_____
((Choices for preparation of sleep are on p. 17)

The Power of Self Care/Self Love: A Journal Workbook Into Your Higher Self

Choose to do something different today.

Today is ___/___/___

In this moment I feel_____

I affirm that I am_____
(Choices of affirmations are on p. 9)

Where can I create joy today? _____
(Choices of joys are on p.11)

I am a House with Four Rooms. I will open and air out each room as a caring and loving gift for myself. (Choices for each are found on p. 13)

Physical_____

Intellectual_____

Emotional _____

Spiritual_____

☾Evening time pondering

What can I look forward to tomorrow?_____

5 things I am thankful for today_____

_____

_____

Sleep revitalizes me. I will prepare for sleep by_____
((Choices for preparation of sleep are on p. 17)

The Power of Self Care/Self Love: A Journal Workbook Into Your Higher Self

Wonder is the beginning of wisdom. -Socrates

Today is ___/___/___

In this moment I feel_____

I affirm that I am_____
(Choices of affirmations are on p. 9)

Where can I create joy today? _____
(Choices of joys are on p.11)

I am a House with Four Rooms. I will open and air out each room as a caring and loving gift for myself. (Choices for each are found on p. 13)

Physical_____

Intellectual_____

Emotional _____

Spiritual_____

🌙 Evening time pondering

What can I look forward to tomorrow?_____

5 things I am thankful for today_____

_____

_____

Sleep revitalizes me. I will prepare for sleep by_____
((Choices for preparation of sleep are on p. 17)

The Power of Self Care/Self Love: A Journal Workbook Into Your Higher Self

Gratitude calms the spirit.

Today is ___/___/___

In this moment I feel_____

I affirm that I am_____
(Choices of affirmations are on p. 9)

Where can I create joy today? _____
(Choices of joys are on p.11)

I am a House with Four Rooms. I will open and air out each room as a caring and loving gift for myself. (Choices for each are found on p. 13)

Physical_____

Intellectual_____

Emotional _____

Spiritual_____

☽Evening time pondering

What can I look forward to tomorrow?_____

5 things I am thankful for today_____

_____

_____

Sleep revitalizes me. I will prepare for sleep by_____
((Choices for preparation of sleep are on p. 17)

This is a brief life, but in its brevity, it offers us some splendid moments, some meaningful adventures
-Rudyard Kipling

What meaningful moments and adventures can you create?

___

___

___

___

___

___

___

___

___

___

The Power of Self Care/Self Love: A Journal Workbook Into Your Higher Self

Let your soul rest in God.

Today is ___/___/___

In this moment I feel_____

I affirm that I am_____
(Choices of affirmations are on p. 9)

Where can I create joy today? _____
(Choices of joys are on p.11)

I am a House with Four Rooms. I will open and air out each room as a caring and loving gift for myself. (Choices for each are found on p. 13)

Physical_____

Intellectual_____

Emotional _____

Spiritual_____

🌙Evening time pondering

What can I look forward to tomorrow?_____

5 things I am thankful for today_____

_____

_____

Sleep revitalizes me. I will prepare for sleep by_____
((Choices for preparation of sleep are on p. 17)

The Power of Self Care/Self Love: A Journal Workbook Into Your Higher Self

What shift are you feeling?

Today is ___/___/___

In this moment I feel_____

I affirm that I am_____
(Choices of affirmations are on p. 9)

Where can I create joy today? _____
(Choices of joys are on p.11)

I am a House with Four Rooms. I will open and air out each room as a caring and loving gift for myself. (Choices for each are found on p. 13)

Physical_____

Intellectual_____

Emotional _____

Spiritual_____

☾Evening time pondering

What can I look forward to tomorrow?_____

5 things I am thankful for today_____

_____

_____

Sleep revitalizes me. I will prepare for sleep by_____
((Choices for preparation of sleep are on p. 17)

What is different today?

Today is ___/___/___

In this moment I feel_____

I affirm that I am_____
(Choices of affirmations are on p. 9)

Where can I create joy today? _____
(Choices of joys are on p.11)

I am a House with Four Rooms. I will open and air out each room as a caring and loving gift for myself. (Choices for each are found on p. 13)

Physical_____

Intellectual_____

Emotional _____

Spiritual_____

☾Evening time pondering

What can I look forward to tomorrow?_____

5 things I am thankful for today_____

_____

_____

Sleep revitalizes me. I will prepare for sleep by_____
((Choices for preparation of sleep are on p. 17)

The Power of Self Care/Self Love: A Journal Workbook Into Your Higher Self

The miracle is this: the more we share the more we have.
-Leonard Nimoy

Today is ___/___/___

In this moment I feel_____

I affirm that I am_____
(Choices of affirmations are on p. 9)

Where can I create joy today? _____
(Choices of joys are on p.11)

I am a House with Four Rooms. I will open and air out each room as a caring and loving gift for myself. (Choices for each are found on p. 13)

Physical_____

Intellectual_____

Emotional _____

Spiritual_____

☾Evening time pondering

What can I look forward to tomorrow?_____

5 things I am thankful for today_____
_____
_____

Sleep revitalizes me. I will prepare for sleep by_____
((Choices for preparation of sleep are on p. 17)

Sometimes, if you are not sure about something, you just have to jump off the bridge and grow your wings on the way down.
-Danielle Steel

Today is ___/___/___

In this moment I feel_____

I affirm that I am_____
(Choices of affirmations are on p. 9)

Where can I create joy today? _____
(Choices of joys are on p.11)

I am a House with Four Rooms. I will open and air out each room as a caring and loving gift for myself. (Choices for each are found on p. 13)

Physical_____

Intellectual_____

Emotional _____

Spiritual_____

☾Evening time pondering

What can I look forward to tomorrow?_____

5 things I am thankful for today_____

_____

_____

Sleep revitalizes me. I will prepare for sleep by_____
((Choices for preparation of sleep are on p. 17)

What Do You Need?

The Power of Self Care/Self Love: A Journal Workbook Into Your Higher Self

Your body is listening to your every thought.

Today is ___/___/___

In this moment I feel_____

I affirm that I am_____
(Choices of affirmations are on p. 9)

Where can I create joy today? _____
(Choices of joys are on p.11)

I am a House with Four Rooms. I will open and air out each room as a caring and loving gift for myself. (Choices for each are found on p. 13)

Physical_____

Intellectual_____

Emotional _____

Spiritual_____

🌙 Evening time pondering

What can I look forward to tomorrow?_____

5 things I am thankful for today_____

_____

_____

Sleep revitalizes me. I will prepare for sleep by_____
((Choices for preparation of sleep are on p. 17)

Life opens up opportunities to you, and you either take them, or you stay afraid of taking them. -Jim Carrey

What opportunities are around you? What opportunities can you create?

_____

_____

_____

_____

_____

_____

_____

_____

_____

_____

_____

_____

_____

The Power of Self Care/Self Love: A Journal Workbook Into Your Higher Self

Today, honor the changes within you.

Today is ___/___/___

In this moment I feel_____

I affirm that I am_____
(Choices of affirmations are on p. 9)

Where can I create joy today? _____
(Choices of joys are on p.11)

I am a House with Four Rooms. I will open and air out each room as a caring and loving gift for myself. (Choices for each are found on p. 13)

Physical_____

Intellectual_____

Emotional _____

Spiritual_____

☾Evening time pondering

What can I look forward to tomorrow?_____

5 things I am thankful for today_____

_____

_____

Sleep revitalizes me. I will prepare for sleep by_____
((Choices for preparation of sleep are on p. 17)

The Power of Self Care/Self Love: A Journal Workbook Into Your Higher Self

The only obstacle is yourself.

Today is ___/___/___

In this moment I feel_____

I affirm that I am_____
(Choices of affirmations are on p. 9)

Where can I create joy today? _____
(Choices of joys are on p.11)

I am a House with Four Rooms. I will open and air out each room as a caring and loving gift for myself. (Choices for each are found on p. 13)

Physical_____

Intellectual_____

Emotional _____

Spiritual_____

🌙Evening time pondering

What can I look forward to tomorrow?_____

5 things I am thankful for today_____

_____

_____

Sleep revitalizes me. I will prepare for sleep by_____
((Choices for preparation of sleep are on p. 17)

The Power of Self Care/Self Love: A Journal Workbook Into Your Higher Self

Today is all that we have. -Louis L'Amour

Today is ___/___/___

In this moment I feel_____

I affirm that I am_____
(Choices of affirmations are on p. 9)

Where can I create joy today? _____
(Choices of joys are on p.11)

I am a House with Four Rooms. I will open and air out each room as a caring and loving gift for myself. (Choices for each are found on p. 13)

Physical_____

Intellectual_____

Emotional _____

Spiritual_____

☽Evening time pondering

What can I look forward to tomorrow?_____

5 things I am thankful for today_____

_____

_____

Sleep revitalizes me. I will prepare for sleep by_____
((Choices for preparation of sleep are on p. 17)

The Power of Self Care/Self Love: A Journal Workbook Into Your Higher Self

You are not an accident.

Today is ___/___/___

In this moment I feel_____

I affirm that I am_____
(Choices of affirmations are on p. 9)

Where can I create joy today? _____
(Choices of joys are on p.11)

I am a House with Four Rooms. I will open and air out each room as a caring and loving gift for myself. (Choices for each are found on p. 13)

Physical_____

Intellectual_____

Emotional _____

Spiritual_____

☾Evening time pondering

What can I look forward to tomorrow?_____

5 things I am thankful for today_____

_____

_____

Sleep revitalizes me. I will prepare for sleep by_____
((Choices for preparation of sleep are on p. 17)

The Power of Self Care/Self Love: A Journal Workbook Into Your Higher Self

Take it all one day at a time and enjoy the journey.
-Kristi Bartlett

Today is ___/___/___

In this moment I feel_____

I affirm that I am_____
(Choices of affirmations are on p. 9)

Where can I create joy today? _____
(Choices of joys are on p.11)

I am a House with Four Rooms. I will open and air out each room as a caring and loving gift for myself. (Choices for each are found on p. 13)

Physical_____

Intellectual_____

Emotional _____

Spiritual_____

☾Evening time pondering

What can I look forward to tomorrow?_____

5 things I am thankful for today_____

_____

_____

Sleep revitalizes me. I will prepare for sleep by_____
((Choices for preparation of sleep are on p. 17)

The Power of Self Care/Self Love: A Journal Workbook Into Your Higher Self

Choose love first.

Today is ___/___/___

In this moment I feel_____

I affirm that I am_____
(Choices of affirmations are on p. 9)

Where can I create joy today? _____
(Choices of joys are on p.11)

I am a House with Four Rooms. I will open and air out each room as a caring and loving gift for myself. (Choices for each are found on p. 13)

Physical_____

Intellectual_____

Emotional _____

Spiritual_____

🌙 Evening time pondering

What can I look forward to tomorrow?_____

5 things I am thankful for today_____

_____

_____

Sleep revitalizes me. I will prepare for sleep by_____
((Choices for preparation of sleep are on p. 17)

Live each day in a state of excited expectancy.
-Reverend Dr. William Augustus Jones Jr

Do you expect things to go wrong? What would today be like if you knew that something wonderful was going to happen? What if you expected this every day? Write your thoughts down.

_____

_____

_____

_____

_____

_____

_____

_____

_____

_____

_____

_____

The Power of Self Care/Self Love: A Journal Workbook Into Your Higher Self

Be kind to yourself.

Today is ___/___/___

In this moment I feel_____

I affirm that I am_____
(Choices of affirmations are on p. 9)

Where can I create joy today? _____
(Choices of joys are on p.11)

I am a House with Four Rooms. I will open and air out each room as a caring and loving gift for myself. (Choices for each are found on p. 13)

Physical_____

Intellectual_____

Emotional _____

Spiritual_____

☾Evening time pondering

What can I look forward to tomorrow?_____

5 things I am thankful for today_____

_____

_____

Sleep revitalizes me. I will prepare for sleep by_____
((Choices for preparation of sleep are on p. 17)

The Power of Self Care/Self Love: A Journal Workbook Into Your Higher Self

Creativity is how we move forward and evolve.

Today is ___/___/___

In this moment I feel_____

I affirm that I am_____
(Choices of affirmations are on p. 9)

Where can I create joy today? _____
(Choices of joys are on p.11)

I am a House with Four Rooms. I will open and air out each room as a caring and loving gift for myself. (Choices for each are found on p. 13)

Physical_____

Intellectual_____

Emotional _____

Spiritual_____

🌙 Evening time pondering

What can I look forward to tomorrow?_____

5 things I am thankful for today_____

_____

_____

Sleep revitalizes me. I will prepare for sleep by_____
((Choices for preparation of sleep are on p. 17)

The Power of Self Care/Self Love: A Journal Workbook Into Your Higher Self

Honor your pain and suffering, then relinquish them.

Today is ___/___/___

In this moment I feel_____

I affirm that I am_____
(Choices of affirmations are on p. 9)

Where can I create joy today? _____
(Choices of joys are on p.11)

I am a House with Four Rooms. I will open and air out each room as a caring and loving gift for myself. (Choices for each are found on p. 13)

Physical_____

Intellectual_____

Emotional _____

Spiritual_____

🌙Evening time pondering

What can I look forward to tomorrow?_____

5 things I am thankful for today_____

_____

_____

Sleep revitalizes me. I will prepare for sleep by_____
((Choices for preparation of sleep are on p. 17)

The Power of Self Care/Self Love: A Journal Workbook Into Your Higher Self

Smile, breathe and go slowly.
-Thich Nhat Hanh

Today is ___/___/___

In this moment I feel_____

I affirm that I am_____
(Choices of affirmations are on p. 9)

Where can I create joy today? _____
(Choices of joys are on p.11)

I am a House with Four Rooms. I will open and air out each room as a caring and loving gift for myself. (Choices for each are found on p. 13)

Physical_____

Intellectual_____

Emotional _____

Spiritual_____

☾Evening time pondering

What can I look forward to tomorrow?_____

5 things I am thankful for today_____

_____

_____

Sleep revitalizes me. I will prepare for sleep by_____
((Choices for preparation of sleep are on p. 17)

Define yourself radically as one beloved by God.
-Brennan Manning

Today is ___/___/___

In this moment I feel_____

I affirm that I am_____
(Choices of affirmations are on p. 9)

Where can I create joy today? _____
(Choices of joys are on p.11)

I am a House with Four Rooms. I will open and air out each room as a caring and loving gift for myself. (Choices for each are found on p. 13)

Physical_____

Intellectual_____

Emotional _____

Spiritual_____

🌙 Evening time pondering

What can I look forward to tomorrow?_____

5 things I am thankful for today_____

_____

_____

Sleep revitalizes me. I will prepare for sleep by_____
((Choices for preparation of sleep are on p. 17)

The Power of Self Care/Self Love: A Journal Workbook Into Your Higher Self

The Power of Self Care/Self Love: A Journal Workbook Into Your Higher Self

Pray and then place all things in God's hands.
– (Mawelita) Carmen Maria Gallindo

Can you be open to trusting a higher energy source to take over?

The Power of Self Care/Self Love: A Journal Workbook Into Your Higher Self

Commit to your soul's desire.

Today is ___/___/___

In this moment I feel_____

I affirm that I am_____
(Choices of affirmations are on p. 9)

Where can I create joy today? _____
(Choices of joys are on p.11)

I am a House with Four Rooms. I will open and air out each room as a caring and loving gift for myself. (Choices for each are found on p. 13)

Physical_____

Intellectual_____

Emotional _____

Spiritual_____

☾ Evening time pondering

What can I look forward to tomorrow?_____

5 things I am thankful for today_____

_____

_____

Sleep revitalizes me. I will prepare for sleep by_____
((Choices for preparation of sleep are on p. 17)

The Power of Self Care/Self Love: A Journal Workbook Into Your Higher Self

Say hello to your inner wisdom.

Today is ___/___/___

In this moment I feel_____

I affirm that I am_____
(Choices of affirmations are on p. 9)

Where can I create joy today?_____
(Choices of joys are on p.11)

I am a House with Four Rooms. I will open and air out each room as a caring and loving gift for myself. (Choices for each are found on p. 13)

Physical_____

Intellectual_____

Emotional _____

Spiritual_____

🌙Evening time pondering

What can I look forward to tomorrow?_____

5 things I am thankful for today_____

_____

_____

Sleep revitalizes me. I will prepare for sleep by_____
((Choices for preparation of sleep are on p. 17)

The Power of Self Care/Self Love: A Journal Workbook Into Your Higher Self

Follow your dreams, transform your life. -Paulo Coelho

Today is ___/___/___

In this moment I feel_____

I affirm that I am_____
(Choices of affirmations are on p. 9)

Where can I create joy today? _____
(Choices of joys are on p.11)

I am a House with Four Rooms. I will open and air out each room as a caring and loving gift for myself. (Choices for each are found on p. 13)

Physical_____

Intellectual_____

Emotional _____

Spiritual_____

☾Evening time pondering

What can I look forward to tomorrow?_____

5 things I am thankful for today_____

_____

_____

Sleep revitalizes me. I will prepare for sleep by_____
((Choices for preparation of sleep are on p. 17)

The Power of Self Care/Self Love: A Journal Workbook Into Your Higher Self

I looked in temples, churches and mosques. But I found the Divine within my heart. -Rumi

Today is ___/___/___

In this moment I feel_____

I affirm that I am_____
(Choices of affirmations are on p. 9)

Where can I create joy today? _____
(Choices of joys are on p.11)

I am a House with Four Rooms. I will open and air out each room as a caring and loving gift for myself. (Choices for each are found on p. 13)

Physical_____

Intellectual_____

Emotional _____

Spiritual_____

☾Evening time pondering

What can I look forward to tomorrow?_____

5 things I am thankful for today_____

_____

_____

Sleep revitalizes me. I will prepare for sleep by_____
((Choices for preparation of sleep are on p. 17)

The Power of Self Care/Self Love: A Journal Workbook Into Your Higher Self

You have all the tools and resources that you need.
-Cherie Carter-Scott

Today is ___/___/___

In this moment I feel_____

I affirm that I am_____
(Choices of affirmations are on p. 9)

Where can I create joy today? _____
(Choices of joys are on p.11)

I am a House with Four Rooms. I will open and air out each room as a caring and loving gift for myself. (Choices for each are found on p. 13)

Physical_____

Intellectual_____

Emotional _____

Spiritual_____

☾Evening time pondering

What can I look forward to tomorrow?_____

5 things I am thankful for today_____

_____

_____

Sleep revitalizes me. I will prepare for sleep by_____
((Choices for preparation of sleep are on p. 17)

The Power of Self Care/Self Love: A Journal Workbook Into Your Higher Self

Trust yourself, you will start to trust others.
-Santosh Kalwar

Today is ___/___/___

In this moment I feel_____

I affirm that I am_____
(Choices of affirmations are on p. 9)

Where can I create joy today? _____
(Choices of joys are on p.11)

I am a House with Four Rooms. I will open and air out each room as a caring and loving gift for myself. (Choices for each are found on p. 13)

Physical_____

Intellectual_____

Emotional _____

Spiritual_____

♪Evening time pondering

What can I look forward to tomorrow?_____

5 things I am thankful for today_____

_____

_____

Sleep revitalizes me. I will prepare for sleep by_____
((Choices for preparation of sleep are on p. 17)

Don't take anything personally. -Don Miguel Ruiz

Your family, partner, kids, friends, and co-workers have their own struggles and issues. What if their unkind words or lack of support did not penetrate you? What if you knew that what they say has nothing to do with you?

The Power of Self Care/Self Love: A Journal Workbook Into Your Higher Self

Your identity is not the work you do or the career you have chosen.

Today is ___/___/___

In this moment I feel_____

I affirm that I am_____
(Choices of affirmations are on p. 9)

Where can I create joy today? _____
(Choices of joys are on p.11)

I am a House with Four Rooms. I will open and air out each room as a caring and loving gift for myself. (Choices for each are found on p. 13)

Physical_____

Intellectual_____

Emotional _____

Spiritual_____

☾Evening time pondering

What can I look forward to tomorrow?_____

5 things I am thankful for today_____

_____

_____

Sleep revitalizes me. I will prepare for sleep by_____
((Choices for preparation of sleep are on p. 17)

The Power of Self Care/Self Love: A Journal Workbook Into Your Higher Self

Laughter is the language of the soul. -Pablo Neruda

Today is ___/___/___

In this moment I feel_____

I affirm that I am_____
(Choices of affirmations are on p. 9)

Where can I create joy today? _____
(Choices of joys are on p.11)

I am a House with Four Rooms. I will open and air out each room as a caring and loving gift for myself. (Choices for each are found on p. 13)

Physical_____

Intellectual_____

Emotional _____

Spiritual_____

☾Evening time pondering

What can I look forward to tomorrow?_____

5 things I am thankful for today_____

_____

_____

Sleep revitalizes me. I will prepare for sleep by_____
((Choices for preparation of sleep are on p. 17)

The Power of Self Care/Self Love: A Journal Workbook Into Your Higher Self

Every truth has two sides. -Aesop

Today is ___/___/___

In this moment I feel_____

I affirm that I am_____
(Choices of affirmations are on p. 9)

Where can I create joy today? _____
(Choices of joys are on p.11)

I am a House with Four Rooms. I will open and air out each room as a caring and loving gift for myself. (Choices for each are found on p. 13)

Physical_____

Intellectual_____

Emotional _____

Spiritual_____

🌙 Evening time pondering

What can I look forward to tomorrow?_____

5 things I am thankful for today_____

_____

_____

Sleep revitalizes me. I will prepare for sleep by_____
((Choices for preparation of sleep are on p. 17)

The Power of Self Care/Self Love: A Journal Workbook Into Your Higher Self

Success is achieved by developing our strengths, not by eliminating our weaknesses. -Marilyn Vos Savant

Today is ___/___/___

In this moment I feel_____

I affirm that I am_____
(Choices of affirmations are on p. 9)

Where can I create joy today? _____
(Choices of joys are on p.11)

I am a House with Four Rooms. I will open and air out each room as a caring and loving gift for myself. (Choices for each are found on p. 13)

Physical_____

Intellectual_____

Emotional _____

Spiritual_____

☾Evening time pondering

What can I look forward to tomorrow?_____

5 things I am thankful for today_____

_____

_____

Sleep revitalizes me. I will prepare for sleep by_____
((Choices for preparation of sleep are on p. 17)

What Do You Need?

The Power of Self Care/Self Love: A Journal Workbook Into Your Higher Self

Life is better when we stay in the present.

Today is ___/___/___

In this moment I feel_____

I affirm that I am_____
(Choices of affirmations are on p. 9)

Where can I create joy today? _____
(Choices of joys are on p.11)

I am a House with Four Rooms. I will open and air out each room as a caring and loving gift for myself. (Choices for each are found on p. 13)

Physical_____

Intellectual_____

Emotional _____

Spiritual_____

🌙Evening time pondering

What can I look forward to tomorrow?_____

5 things I am thankful for today_____

_____

_____

Sleep revitalizes me. I will prepare for sleep by_____
((Choices for preparation of sleep are on p. 17)

The Power of Self Care/Self Love: A Journal Workbook Into Your Higher Self

You are healing.

Today is ___/___/___

In this moment I feel_____

I affirm that I am_____
(Choices of affirmations are on p. 9)

Where can I create joy today? _____
(Choices of joys are on p.11)

I am a House with Four Rooms. I will open and air out each room as a caring and loving gift for myself. (Choices for each are found on p. 13)

Physical_____

Intellectual_____

Emotional _____

Spiritual_____

☾Evening time pondering

What can I look forward to tomorrow?_____

5 things I am thankful for today_____

_____

_____

Sleep revitalizes me. I will prepare for sleep by_____
((Choices for preparation of sleep are on p. 17)

The Power of Self Care/Self Love: A Journal Workbook Into Your Higher Self

Doing something rather than nothing paves a path for good to follow.

Today is ___/___/___

In this moment I feel_____

I affirm that I am_____
(Choices of affirmations are on p. 9)

Where can I create joy today?_____
(Choices of joys are on p.11)

I am a House with Four Rooms. I will open and air out each room as a caring and loving gift for myself. (Choices for each are found on p. 13)

Physical_____

Intellectual_____

Emotional _____

Spiritual_____

☾Evening time pondering

What can I look forward to tomorrow?_____

5 things I am thankful for today_____

_____

_____

Sleep revitalizes me. I will prepare for sleep by_____
((Choices for preparation of sleep are on p. 17)

The Power of Self Care/Self Love: A Journal Workbook Into Your Higher Self

Count your age by friends, not years. Count your life by smiles, not tears -John Lennon

Today is ___/___/___

In this moment I feel_____

I affirm that I am_____
(Choices of affirmations are on p. 9)

Where can I create joy today?_____
(Choices of joys are on p.11)

I am a House with Four Rooms. I will open and air out each room as a caring and loving gift for myself. (Choices for each are found on p. 13)

Physical_____

Intellectual_____

Emotional _____

Spiritual_____

🌙 Evening time pondering

What can I look forward to tomorrow?_____

5 things I am thankful for today_____

_____

_____

Sleep revitalizes me. I will prepare for sleep by_____
((Choices for preparation of sleep are on p. 17)

Have compassion for yourself

List 5 things that you have accomplished in your life. Were they easy to achieve? Go back and put what you had to do to achieve them. Look at this list and have compassion for the hard work, time and sacrifice it took. In this moment honor the journey that you have already taken. What would today be like if you removed self-judgement and honored the wonderful being that you are?

_____

_____

_____

_____

_____

_____

_____

_____

_____

_____

The Power of Self Care/Self Love: A Journal Workbook Into Your Higher Self

I don't believe, I know. -Carl Jung

Today is ___/___/___

In this moment I feel_____

I affirm that I am_____
(Choices of affirmations are on p. 9)

Where can I create joy today?_____
(Choices of joys are on p.11)

I am a House with Four Rooms. I will open and air out each room as a caring and loving gift for myself. (Choices for each are found on p. 13)

Physical_____

Intellectual_____

Emotional _____

Spiritual_____

☽Evening time pondering

What can I look forward to tomorrow?_____

5 things I am thankful for today_____

_____

_____

Sleep revitalizes me. I will prepare for sleep by_____
((Choices for preparation of sleep are on p. 17)

What is the worst that could happen?

Today is ___/___/___

In this moment I feel_____

I affirm that I am_____
(Choices of affirmations are on p. 9)

Where can I create joy today?_____
(Choices of joys are on p.11)

I am a House with Four Rooms. I will open and air out each room as a caring and loving gift for myself. (Choices for each are found on p. 13)

Physical_____

Intellectual_____

Emotional _____

Spiritual_____

☾Evening time pondering

What can I look forward to tomorrow?_____

5 things I am thankful for today_____

_____

_____

Sleep revitalizes me. I will prepare for sleep by_____
((Choices for preparation of sleep are on p. 17)

The Power of Self Care/Self Love: A Journal Workbook Into Your Higher Self

Angels can fly because they take themselves lightly.
-G.K. Chesterton

Today is ___/___/___

In this moment I feel_____

I affirm that I am_____
(Choices of affirmations are on p. 9)

Where can I create joy today?_____
(Choices of joys are on p.11)

I am a House with Four Rooms. I will open and air out each room as a caring and loving gift for myself. (Choices for each are found on p. 13)

Physical_____

Intellectual_____

Emotional _____

Spiritual_____

☾Evening time pondering

What can I look forward to tomorrow?_____

5 things I am thankful for today_____
_____
_____

Sleep revitalizes me. I will prepare for sleep by_____
((Choices for preparation of sleep are on p. 17)

The Power of Self Care/Self Love: A Journal Workbook Into Your Higher Self

Our lives are the evolution of our stanzas and spaces all going through a metamorphosis, coming out of a cocoon, revealing a masterpiece, YOU!

Today is ___/___/___

In this moment I feel_____

I affirm that I am_____
(Choices of affirmations are on p. 9)

Where can I create joy today?_____
(Choices of joys are on p.11)

I am a House with Four Rooms. I will open and air out each room as a caring and loving gift for myself. (Choices for each are found on p. 13)

Physical_____

Intellectual_____

Emotional _____

Spiritual_____

🌙 Evening time pondering

What can I look forward to tomorrow?_____

5 things I am thankful for today_____

_____

_____

Sleep revitalizes me. I will prepare for sleep by_____
((Choices for preparation of sleep are on p. 17)

The Power of Self Care/Self Love: A Journal Workbook Into Your Higher Self

When you put your health first, every cell in your body has a thank you party!

Today is ___/___/___

In this moment I feel_____

I affirm that I am_____
(Choices of affirmations are on p. 9)

Where can I create joy today?_____
(Choices of joys are on p.11)

I am a House with Four Rooms. I will open and air out each room as a caring and loving gift for myself. (Choices for each are found on p. 13)

Physical_____

Intellectual_____

Emotional _____

Spiritual_____

🌙 Evening time pondering

What can I look forward to tomorrow?_____

5 things I am thankful for today_____

_____

_____

Sleep revitalizes me. I will prepare for sleep by_____
((Choices for preparation of sleep are on p. 17)

look for the gifts each season brings you.

Depending on where you live, the temperatures change with the seasons. Are you enjoying the season that you are in? Can you place something on your kitchen table that represents the joy that this season brings? Write down how you feel during this season. Any memories?

_____

_____

_____

_____

_____

_____

_____

_____

_____

_____

The Power of Self Care/Self Love: A Journal Workbook Into Your Higher Self

I learned that you can't truly own anything, that true ownership comes only in the moment of giving. -Mia Farrow

Today is ___/___/___

In this moment I feel_____

I affirm that I am_____
(Choices of affirmations are on p. 9)

Where can I create joy today?_____
(Choices of joys are on p.11)

I am a House with Four Rooms. I will open and air out each room as a caring and loving gift for myself. (Choices for each are found on p. 13)

Physical_____

Intellectual_____

Emotional _____

Spiritual_____

☾Evening time pondering

What can I look forward to tomorrow?_____

5 things I am thankful for today_____

_____

_____

Sleep revitalizes me. I will prepare for sleep by_____
((Choices for preparation of sleep are on p. 17)

The Power of Self Care/Self Love: A Journal Workbook Into Your Higher Self

You have the ability to create, grow, and move forward.

Today is ___/___/___

In this moment I feel_____

I affirm that I am_____
(Choices of affirmations are on p. 9)

Where can I create joy today?_____
(Choices of joys are on p.11)

I am a House with Four Rooms. I will open and air out each room as a caring and loving gift for myself. (Choices for each are found on p. 13)

Physical_____

Intellectual_____

Emotional _____

Spiritual_____

☾Evening time pondering

What can I look forward to tomorrow?_____

5 things I am thankful for today_____

_____

_____

Sleep revitalizes me. I will prepare for sleep by_____
((Choices for preparation of sleep are on p. 17)

The Power of Self Care/Self Love: A Journal Workbook Into Your Higher Self

Scientists have demonstrated that there may be...
a life force flowing through the universe...collective
consciousness...theologians...term it, the Holy Spirit.
-Lynn McTaggart

Today is ___/___/___

In this moment I feel_____

I affirm that I am_____
(Choices of affirmations are on p. 9)

Where can I create joy today?_____
(Choices of joys are on p.11)

I am a House with Four Rooms. I will open and air out each room as a caring and loving gift for myself. (Choices for each are found on p. 13)

Physical_____

Intellectual_____

Emotional_____

Spiritual_____

☾Evening time pondering

What can I look forward to tomorrow?_____

5 things I am thankful for today_____

_____

_____

Sleep revitalizes me. I will prepare for sleep by_____
((Choices for preparation of sleep are on p. 17)

The Power of Self Care/Self Love: A Journal Workbook Into Your Higher Self

Me Time + Moving Your Body= Active Self Time (AST)

Today is ___/___/___

In this moment I feel_____

I affirm that I am_____
(Choices of affirmations are on p. 9)

Where can I create joy today?_____
(Choices of joys are on p.11)

I am a House with Four Rooms. I will open and air out each room as a caring and loving gift for myself. (Choices for each are found on p. 13)

Physical_____

Intellectual_____

Emotional _____

Spiritual_____

☽Evening time pondering

What can I look forward to tomorrow?_____

5 things I am thankful for today_____

_____

_____

Sleep revitalizes me. I will prepare for sleep by_____
((Choices for preparation of sleep are on p. 17)

What Do You Need?

The Power of Self Care/Self Love: A Journal Workbook Into Your Higher Self

Find the courage to ask questions, and to express what you really want. -Don Miguel Ruiz

Today is ___/___/___

In this moment I feel_____

I affirm that I am_____
(Choices of affirmations are on p. 9)

Where can I create joy today?_____
(Choices of joys are on p.11)

I am a House with Four Rooms. I will open and air out each room as a caring and loving gift for myself. (Choices for each are found on p. 13)

Physical_____

Intellectual_____

Emotional _____

Spiritual_____

☾Evening time pondering

What can I look forward to tomorrow?_____

5 things I am thankful for today_____

_____

_____

Sleep revitalizes me. I will prepare for sleep by_____
((Choices for preparation of sleep are on p. 17)

The Power of Self Care/Self Love: A Journal Workbook Into Your Higher Self

There is no way to happiness-happiness is the way.
-Thich Nhat Hanh

Today is ___/___/___

In this moment I feel_____

I affirm that I am_____
(Choices of affirmations are on p. 9)

Where can I create joy today?_____
(Choices of joys are on p.11)

I am a House with Four Rooms. I will open and air out each room as a caring and loving gift for myself. (Choices for each are found on p. 13)

Physical_____

Intellectual_____

Emotional _____

Spiritual_____

🌙 Evening time pondering

What can I look forward to tomorrow?_____

5 things I am thankful for today_____

_____

_____

Sleep revitalizes me. I will prepare for sleep by_____
((Choices for preparation of sleep are on p. 17)

The Power of Self Care/Self Love: A Journal Workbook Into Your Higher Self

What makes you different, or weird, that's your strength.
-Meryl Streep

Today is ___/___/___

In this moment I feel_____

I affirm that I am_____
(Choices of affirmations are on p. 9)

Where can I create joy today?_____
(Choices of joys are on p.11)

I am a House with Four Rooms. I will open and air out each room as a caring and loving gift for myself. (Choices for each are found on p. 13)

Physical_____

Intellectual_____

Emotional _____

Spiritual_____

☾Evening time pondering

What can I look forward to tomorrow?_____

5 things I am thankful for today_____

_____

_____

Sleep revitalizes me. I will prepare for sleep by_____
((Choices for preparation of sleep are on p. 17)

The Power of Self Care/Self Love: A Journal Workbook Into Your Higher Self

If we understood the power of our thoughts, we would guard them more closely. -Betty Eadie

Today is ___/___/___

In this moment I feel_____

I affirm that I am_____
(Choices of affirmations are on p. 9)

Where can I create joy today?_____
(Choices of joys are on p.11)

I am a House with Four Rooms. I will open and air out each room as a caring and loving gift for myself. (Choices for each are found on p. 13)

Physical_____

Intellectual_____

Emotional _____

Spiritual_____

☾Evening time pondering

What can I look forward to tomorrow?_____

5 things I am thankful for today_____
_____
_____

Sleep revitalizes me. I will prepare for sleep by_____
((Choices for preparation of sleep are on p. 17)

Your well-being depends on you.

Depending on others to keep you happy and healthy will over burden those you love. List here the ways you can create joy, happiness and a healthy mind, body, and spirit. Which one can you start today?

_____

_____

_____

_____

_____

_____

_____

_____

_____

_____

_____

_____

The Power of Self Care/Self Love: A Journal Workbook Into Your Higher Self

Open your heart to infinite love.

Today is ___/___/___

In this moment I feel_____

I affirm that I am_____
(Choices of affirmations are on p. 9)

Where can I create joy today?_____
(Choices of joys are on p.11)

I am a House with Four Rooms. I will open and air out each room as a caring and loving gift for myself. (Choices for each are found on p. 13)

Physical_____

Intellectual_____

Emotional _____

Spiritual_____

☾Evening time pondering

What can I look forward to tomorrow?_____

5 things I am thankful for today_____

_____

_____

Sleep revitalizes me. I will prepare for sleep by_____
((Choices for preparation of sleep are on p. 17)

The Power of Self Care/Self Love: A Journal Workbook Into Your Higher Self

Follow your bliss. -Joseph Campbell

Today is ___/___/___

In this moment I feel_____

I affirm that I am_____
(Choices of affirmations are on p. 9)

Where can I create joy today?_____
(Choices of joys are on p.11)

I am a House with Four Rooms. I will open and air out each room as a caring and loving gift for myself. (Choices for each are found on p. 13)

Physical_____

Intellectual_____

Emotional _____

Spiritual_____

☾Evening time pondering

What can I look forward to tomorrow?_____

5 things I am thankful for today_____

_____

_____

Sleep revitalizes me. I will prepare for sleep by_____
((Choices for preparation of sleep are on p. 17)

The Power of Self Care/Self Love: A Journal Workbook Into Your Higher Self

You are the average of who you spend the most time with.
–Jim Rohn

Today is ___/___/___

In this moment I feel_____

I affirm that I am_____
(Choices of affirmations are on p. 9)

Where can I create joy today?_____
(Choices of joys are on p.11)

I am a House with Four Rooms. I will open and air out each room as a caring and loving gift for myself. (Choices for each are found on p. 13)

Physical_____

Intellectual_____

Emotional _____

Spiritual_____

☾Evening time pondering

What can I look forward to tomorrow?_____

5 things I am thankful for today_____

_____

_____

Sleep revitalizes me. I will prepare for sleep by_____
((Choices for preparation of sleep are on p. 17)

The Power of Self Care/Self Love: A Journal Workbook Into Your Higher Self

We need twelve hugs a day for growth. -Virginia Satir

Today is ___/___/___

In this moment I feel_____

I affirm that I am_____
(Choices of affirmations are on p. 9)

Where can I create joy today?_____
(Choices of joys are on p.11)

I am a House with Four Rooms. I will open and air out each room as a caring and loving gift for myself. (Choices for each are found on p. 13)

Physical_____

Intellectual_____

Emotional _____

Spiritual_____

☾Evening time pondering

What can I look forward to tomorrow?_____

5 things I am thankful for today_____

_____

_____

Sleep revitalizes me. I will prepare for sleep by_____
((Choices for preparation of sleep are on p. 17)

The Power of Self Care/Self Love: A Journal Workbook Into Your Higher Self

We need joy as we need air. -Maya Angelou

Today is ___/___/___

In this moment I feel_____

I affirm that I am_____
(Choices of affirmations are on p. 9)

Where can I create joy today?_____
(Choices of joys are on p.11)

I am a House with Four Rooms. I will open and air out each room as a caring and loving gift for myself. (Choices for each are found on p. 13)

Physical_____

Intellectual_____

Emotional _____

Spiritual_____

☾Evening time pondering

What can I look forward to tomorrow?_____

5 things I am thankful for today_____

_____

_____

Sleep revitalizes me. I will prepare for sleep by_____
((Choices for preparation of sleep are on p. 17)

The Power of Self Care/Self Love: A Journal Workbook Into Your Higher Self

Dreams become reality when we put our minds to it.
-Queen Latifah

Today is ___/___/___

In this moment I feel_____

I affirm that I am_____
(Choices of affirmations are on p. 9)

Where can I create joy today?_____
(Choices of joys are on p.11)

I am a House with Four Rooms. I will open and air out each room as a caring and loving gift for myself. (Choices for each are found on p. 13)

Physical_____

Intellectual_____

Emotional _____

Spiritual_____

🌙Evening time pondering

What can I look forward to tomorrow?_____

5 things I am thankful for today_____

_____

_____

Sleep revitalizes me. I will prepare for sleep by_____
((Choices for preparation of sleep are on p. 17)

Plan your next vacation.

Time away from work and family rejuvenates your soul. Where would you like to go? Can you take or request a week off in 3, 6 months or a year? Put it on your calendar and begin to dream of your destination. Write your ideas on this page. Buy your ticket.

The Power of Self Care/Self Love: A Journal Workbook Into Your Higher Self

The only obstacle to your evolving is yourself.

Today is ___/___/___

In this moment I feel_____

I affirm that I am_____
(Choices of affirmations are on p. 9)

Where can I create joy today?_____
(Choices of joys are on p.11)

I am a House with Four Rooms. I will open and air out each room as a caring and loving gift for myself. (Choices for each are found on p. 13)

Physical_____

Intellectual_____

Emotional _____

Spiritual_____

☾Evening time pondering

What can I look forward to tomorrow?_____

5 things I am thankful for today_____

_____

_____

Sleep revitalizes me. I will prepare for sleep by_____
((Choices for preparation of sleep are on p. 17)

The Power of Self Care/Self Love: A Journal Workbook Into Your Higher Self

You are Enough. -Sierra Boggess

Today is ___/___/___

In this moment I feel_____

I affirm that I am_____
(Choices of affirmations are on p. 9)

Where can I create joy today?_____
(Choices of joys are on p.11)

I am a House with Four Rooms. I will open and air out each room as a caring and loving gift for myself. (Choices for each are found on p. 13)

Physical_____

Intellectual_____

Emotional _____

Spiritual_____

☾Evening time pondering

What can I look forward to tomorrow?_____

5 things I am thankful for today_____

_____

_____

Sleep revitalizes me. I will prepare for sleep by_____
((Choices for preparation of sleep are on p. 17)

The Power of Self Care/Self Love: A Journal Workbook Into Your Higher Self

Tell the truth, work hard, and come to dinner on time.
-Gerald Ford

Today is ___/___/___

In this moment I feel_____

I affirm that I am_____
(Choices of affirmations are on p. 9)

Where can I create joy today?_____
(Choices of joys are on p.11)

I am a House with Four Rooms. I will open and air out each room as a caring and loving gift for myself. (Choices for each are found on p. 13)

Physical_____

Intellectual_____

Emotional _____

Spiritual_____

🌙Evening time pondering

What can I look forward to tomorrow?_____

5 things I am thankful for today_____

_____

_____

Sleep revitalizes me. I will prepare for sleep by_____
((Choices for preparation of sleep are on p. 17)

The Power of Self Care/Self Love: A Journal Workbook Into Your Higher Self

The Power of Self Care/Self Love: A Journal Workbook Into Your Higher Self

There is wonder in today.

Today is ___/___/___

In this moment I feel_____

I affirm that I am_____
(Choices of affirmations are on p. 9)

Where can I create joy today?_____
(Choices of joys are on p.11)

I am a House with Four Rooms. I will open and air out each room as a caring and loving gift for myself. (Choices for each are found on p. 13)

Physical_____

Intellectual_____

Emotional _____

Spiritual_____

☾Evening time pondering

What can I look forward to tomorrow?_____

5 things I am thankful for today_____

_____

_____

Sleep revitalizes me. I will prepare for sleep by_____
((Choices for preparation of sleep are on p. 17)

The Power of Self Care/Self Love: A Journal Workbook Into Your Higher Self

Stay in shape .-Mohammed Ali's last words to his grandson.

Today is ___/___/___

In this moment I feel_____

I affirm that I am_____
(Choices of affirmations are on p. 9)

Where can I create joy today?_____
(Choices of joys are on p.11)

I am a House with Four Rooms. I will open and air out each room as a caring and loving gift for myself. (Choices for each are found on p. 13)

Physical_____

Intellectual_____

Emotional _____

Spiritual_____

☾Evening time pondering

What can I look forward to tomorrow?_____

5 things I am thankful for today_____

_____

_____

Sleep revitalizes me. I will prepare for sleep by_____
((Choices for preparation of sleep are on p. 17)

Gratitude is the key to happiness.

Go ahead and fill this page up with everything you are grateful for. Gratitude opens the doors to receiving more of what you need.

_____

_____

_____

_____

_____

_____

_____

_____

_____

_____

_____

_____

_____

_____

We are spiritual beings having a human experience.
-Pierre Teilhard de Chardin

Today is ___/___/___

In this moment I feel_____

I affirm that I am_____
(Choices of affirmations are on p. 9)

Where can I create joy today?_____
(Choices of joys are on p.11)

I am a House with Four Rooms. I will open and air out each room as a caring and loving gift for myself. (Choices for each are found on p. 13)

Physical_____

Intellectual_____

Emotional _____

Spiritual_____

🌙 Evening time pondering

What can I look forward to tomorrow?_____

5 things I am thankful for today_____

_____

_____

Sleep revitalizes me. I will prepare for sleep by_____
((Choices for preparation of sleep are on p. 17)

What Do You Need?

The Power of Self Care/Self Love: A Journal Workbook Into Your Higher Self

Choose wisely who sits at your round table.

Today is ___/___/___

In this moment I feel_____

I affirm that I am_____
(Choices of affirmations are on p. 9)

Where can I create joy today?_____
(Choices of joys are on p.11)

I am a House with Four Rooms. I will open and air out each room as a caring and loving gift for myself. (Choices for each are found on p. 13)

Physical_____

Intellectual_____

Emotional _____

Spiritual_____

☾Evening time pondering

What can I look forward to tomorrow?_____

5 things I am thankful for today_____

_____

_____

Sleep revitalizes me. I will prepare for sleep by_____
((Choices for preparation of sleep are on p. 17)

The Power of Self Care/Self Love: A Journal Workbook Into Your Higher Self

We cannot become who we need to be by remaining who we are. -Max DePree

Today is ___/___/___

In this moment I feel_____

I affirm that I am_____
(Choices of affirmations are on p. 9)

Where can I create joy today?_____
(Choices of joys are on p.11)

I am a House with Four Rooms. I will open and air out each room as a caring and loving gift for myself. (Choices for each are found on p. 13)

Physical_____

Intellectual_____

Emotional _____

Spiritual_____

☾Evening time pondering

What can I look forward to tomorrow?_____

5 things I am thankful for today_____

_____

_____

Sleep revitalizes me. I will prepare for sleep by_____
((Choices for preparation of sleep are on p. 17)

The Power of Self Care/Self Love: A Journal Workbook Into Your Higher Self

People will forget what you said, people will forget what you did, but people will never forget how you made them feel.
-Maya Angelou

Today is ___/___/___

In this moment I feel_____

I affirm that I am_____
(Choices of affirmations are on p. 9)

Where can I create joy today?_____
(Choices of joys are on p.11)

I am a House with Four Rooms. I will open and air out each room as a caring and loving gift for myself. (Choices for each are found on p. 13)

Physical_____

Intellectual_____

Emotional _____

Spiritual_____

🌙Evening time pondering

What can I look forward to tomorrow?_____

5 things I am thankful for today_____

_____

_____

Sleep revitalizes me. I will prepare for sleep by_____
((Choices for preparation of sleep are on p. 17)

With the new day comes new strengths and new thoughts.
-Eleanor Roosevelt

Today is ___/___/___

In this moment I feel_____

I affirm that I am_____
(Choices of affirmations are on p. 9)

Where can I create joy today?_____
(Choices of joys are on p.11)

I am a House with Four Rooms. I will open and air out each room as a caring and loving gift for myself. (Choices for each are found on p. 13)

Physical_____

Intellectual_____

Emotional_____

Spiritual_____

☽Evening time pondering

What can I look forward to tomorrow?_____

5 things I am thankful for today_____

_____

_____

Sleep revitalizes me. I will prepare for sleep by_____
((Choices for preparation of sleep are on p. 17)

Life is 10% what happens to you and 90% how you react to it. -Charles Swindoll

What is happening in your life right now that you wish was not occurring? How can you react to it in a way that is more positive and productive for yourself?

_____

_____

_____

_____

_____

_____

_____

_____

_____

_____

_____

_____

The Power of Self Care/Self Love: A Journal Workbook Into Your Higher Self

The best is yet to come. -William Shakespeare

Today is ___/___/___

In this moment I feel_____

I affirm that I am_____
(Choices of affirmations are on p. 9)

Where can I create joy today?_____
(Choices of joys are on p.11)

I am a House with Four Rooms. I will open and air out each room as a caring and loving gift for myself. (Choices for each are found on p. 13)

Physical_____

Intellectual_____

Emotional _____

Spiritual_____

☾Evening time pondering

What can I look forward to tomorrow?_____

5 things I am thankful for today_____

_____

_____

Sleep revitalizes me. I will prepare for sleep by_____
((Choices for preparation of sleep are on p. 17)

The Power of Self Care/Self Love: A Journal Workbook Into Your Higher Self

From what we get, we can make a living; what we give, however, makes a life.
-Arthur Ashe

Today is ___/___/___

In this moment I feel_____

I affirm that I am_____
(Choices of affirmations are on p. 9)

Where can I create joy today?_____
(Choices of joys are on p.11)

I am a House with Four Rooms. I will open and air out each room as a caring and loving gift for myself. (Choices for each are found on p. 13)

Physical_____

Intellectual_____

Emotional _____

Spiritual_____

☽Evening time pondering

What can I look forward to tomorrow?_____

5 things I am thankful for today_____

_____

_____

Sleep revitalizes me. I will prepare for sleep by_____
((Choices for preparation of sleep are on p. 17)

The Power of Self Care/Self Love: A Journal Workbook Into Your Higher Self

In daily life we must see that it is not happiness that makes us grateful, but gratefulness that makes us happy.
-Brother David Steindl-Rast

Today is ___/___/___

In this moment I feel_____

I affirm that I am_____
(Choices of affirmations are on p. 9)

Where can I create joy today?_____
(Choices of joys are on p.11)

I am a House with Four Rooms. I will open and air out each room as a caring and loving gift for myself. (Choices for each are found on p. 13)

Physical_____

Intellectual_____

Emotional _____

Spiritual_____

☾Evening time pondering

What can I look forward to tomorrow?_____

5 things I am thankful for today_____

_____

_____

Sleep revitalizes me. I will prepare for sleep by_____
((Choices for preparation of sleep are on p. 17)

The Power of Self Care/Self Love: A Journal Workbook Into Your Higher Self

Empowered Women Empower Women. -unknown

Today is ___/___/___

In this moment I feel_____

I affirm that I am_____
(Choices of affirmations are on p. 9)

Where can I create joy today?_____
(Choices of joys are on p.11)

I am a House with Four Rooms. I will open and air out each room as a caring and loving gift for myself. (Choices for each are found on p. 13)

Physical_____

Intellectual_____

Emotional _____

Spiritual_____

☾Evening time pondering

What can I look forward to tomorrow?_____

5 things I am thankful for today_____

_____

_____

Sleep revitalizes me. I will prepare for sleep by_____
((Choices for preparation of sleep are on p. 17)

Surround yourself only with people who are going to take you higher. -Oprah Winfrey

Who are the knights at your round table? Who is your cheerleader? Who tells you the truth with kindness? Who is there with you when you are at your lowest? Who thinks you are great?

_____

_____

_____

_____

_____

_____

_____

_____

_____

_____

The Power of Self Care/Self Love: A Journal Workbook Into Your Higher Self

When they go low, we go high.
-Michelle Obama

Today is ___/___/___

In this moment I feel_____

I affirm that I am_____
(Choices of affirmations are on p. 9)

Where can I create joy today?_____
(Choices of joys are on p.11)

I am a House with Four Rooms. I will open and air out each room as a caring and loving gift for myself. (Choices for each are found on p. 13)

Physical_____

Intellectual_____

Emotional _____

Spiritual_____

🌙Evening time pondering

What can I look forward to tomorrow?_____

5 things I am thankful for today_____

_____

_____

Sleep revitalizes me. I will prepare for sleep by_____
((Choices for preparation of sleep are on p. 17)

The Power of Self Care/Self Love: A Journal Workbook Into Your Higher Self

Experience love in yourself and others.

Today is ___/___/___

In this moment I feel_____

I affirm that I am_____
(Choices of affirmations are on p. 9)

Where can I create joy today?_____
(Choices of joys are on p.11)

I am a House with Four Rooms. I will open and air out each room as a caring and loving gift for myself. (Choices for each are found on p. 13)

Physical_____

Intellectual_____

Emotional _____

Spiritual_____

☾Evening time pondering

What can I look forward to tomorrow?_____

5 things I am thankful for today_____

_____

_____

Sleep revitalizes me. I will prepare for sleep by_____
((Choices for preparation of sleep are on p. 17)

The Power of Self Care/Self Love: A Journal Workbook Into Your Higher Self

The most common way people give up their power is by thinking they do not have any. -Alice Walker

Today is ___/___/___

In this moment I feel_____

I affirm that I am_____
(Choices of affirmations are on p. 9)

Where can I create joy today?_____
(Choices of joys are on p.11)

I am a House with Four Rooms. I will open and air out each room as a caring and loving gift for myself. (Choices for each are found on p. 13)

Physical_____

Intellectual_____

Emotional _____

Spiritual_____

🌙 Evening time pondering

What can I look forward to tomorrow?_____

5 things I am thankful for today_____

_____

_____

Sleep revitalizes me. I will prepare for sleep by_____
((Choices for preparation of sleep are on p. 17)

Vision Board #2:
Places I Would Love to Visit

It's been 180 days and it's time to indulge yourself and do some armchair traveling, your second vision board.

Like a scavenger hunt, look for what you have cut out or printed and taped to the last 10 pages. Are there towns, cities, countries, beaches, lakes, rivers, waterfalls, mountains, or national parks you would love to visit? If you have not yet found much to represent these places, then take some time today to explore travel magazines, newspapers, Pinterest, or Canva and cut out and print your items on an 11x14 (or larger) cork board, thick poster board, magnetic dry erase board, or canvas.

There are no rules, just a fun exploration of where your body, mind and spirit want to go.

Vision boards can have:
sticky notes
Colored paper sheets
3x5 index cards
A poem
Well-thought-out typed words
Pictures of what you love
Real pictures of you, family, friends

Remember this is a fun activity so grab your scissors, glue, scotch tape, markers, push pins or magnets.

The Power of Self Care/Self Love: A Journal Workbook Into Your Higher Self

You get in life what you have the courage to ask for.
-Oprah Winfrey

Today is ___/___/___

In this moment I feel_____

I affirm that I am_____
(Choices of affirmations are on p. 9)

Where can I create joy today?_____
(Choices of joys are on p.11)

I am a House with Four Rooms. I will open and air out each room as a caring and loving gift for myself. (Choices for each are found on p. 13)

Physical_____

Intellectual_____

Emotional _____

Spiritual_____

🌙 Evening time pondering

What can I look forward to tomorrow?_____

5 things I am thankful for today_____
_____
_____

Sleep revitalizes me. I will prepare for sleep by_____
((Choices for preparation of sleep are on p. 17)

What Do You Need?

The Power of Self Care/Self Love: A Journal Workbook Into Your Higher Self

If you want to change the world, go home and love your family
-Mother Teresa

Today is ___/___/___

In this moment I feel_____

I affirm that I am_____
(Choices of affirmations are on p. 9)

Where can I create joy today?_____
(Choices of joys are on p.11)

I am a House with Four Rooms. I will open and air out each room as a caring and loving gift for myself. (Choices for each are found on p. 13)

Physical_____

Intellectual_____

Emotional _____

Spiritual_____

☽ Evening time pondering

What can I look forward to tomorrow?_____

5 things I am thankful for today_____

_____

_____

Sleep revitalizes me. I will prepare for sleep by_____
((Choices for preparation of sleep are on p. 17)

The Power of Self Care/Self Love: A Journal Workbook Into Your Higher Self

Love makes your soul climb out of its hiding place.
-Zora Neale Hurston

Today is ___/___/___

In this moment I feel_____

I affirm that I am_____
(Choices of affirmations are on p. 9)

Where can I create joy today?_____
(Choices of joys are on p.11)

I am a House with Four Rooms. I will open and air out each room as a caring and loving gift for myself. (Choices for each are found on p. 13)

Physical_____

Intellectual_____

Emotional _____

Spiritual_____

☾Evening time pondering

What can I look forward to tomorrow?_____

5 things I am thankful for today_____

_____

_____

Sleep revitalizes me. I will prepare for sleep by_____
((Choices for preparation of sleep are on p. 17)

If you want to fly, you have to give up everything that weighs you down. –Toni Morrison

Sometimes your own worst enemy is yourself. Listen to the judgemental words we all use: "I'm not good enough. I'm not smart enough." Occasionally, we hold onto our past lives, or unsupportive friends and family. What do you need to give up to move forward and fly?

_____

_____

_____

_____

_____

_____

_____

_____

_____

_____

_____

_____

*To have self-esteem is truly an act of revolution,
and our revolution is long overdue.*
-Margaret Cho

Today is ___/___/___

In this moment I feel_____

I affirm that I am_____
(Choices of affirmations are on p. 9)

Where can I create joy today?_____
(Choices of joys are on p.11)

I am a House with Four Rooms. I will open and air out each room as a caring and loving gift for myself. (Choices for each are found on p. 13)

Physical_____

Intellectual_____

Emotional _____

Spiritual_____

☾Evening time pondering

What can I look forward to tomorrow?_____

5 things I am thankful for today_____

_____

_____

Sleep revitalizes me. I will prepare for sleep by_____
((Choices for preparation of sleep are on p. 17)

The Power of Self Care/Self Love: A Journal Workbook Into Your Higher Self

Some cause happiness wherever they go; others whenever they go
-Oscar Wilde

Today is ___/___/___

In this moment I feel_____

I affirm that I am_____
(Choices of affirmations are on p. 9)

Where can I create joy today?_____
(Choices of joys are on p.11)

I am a House with Four Rooms. I will open and air out each room as a caring and loving gift for myself. (Choices for each are found on p. 13)

Physical_____

Intellectual_____

Emotional _____

Spiritual_____

🌙Evening time pondering

What can I look forward to tomorrow?_____

5 things I am thankful for today_____

_____

_____

Sleep revitalizes me. I will prepare for sleep by_____
((Choices for preparation of sleep are on p. 17)

The Power of Self Care/Self Love: A Journal Workbook Into Your Higher Self

Just do the work and trust the work.
-John F. Barnes

Today is ___/___/___

In this moment I feel_____

I affirm that I am_____
(Choices of affirmations are on p. 9)

Where can I create joy today?_____
(Choices of joys are on p.11)

I am a House with Four Rooms. I will open and air out each room as a caring and loving gift for myself. (Choices for each are found on p. 13)

Physical_____

Intellectual_____

Emotional _____

Spiritual _____

☾Evening time pondering

What can I look forward to tomorrow?_____

5 things I am thankful for today_____

_____

_____

Sleep revitalizes me. I will prepare for sleep by_____
((Choices for preparation of sleep are on p. 17)

The Power of Self Care/Self Love: A Journal Workbook Into Your Higher Self

Your best is good enough.

Today is ___/___/___

In this moment I feel_____

I affirm that I am_____
(Choices of affirmations are on p. 9)

Where can I create joy today?_____
(Choices of joys are on p.11)

I am a House with Four Rooms. I will open and air out each room as a caring and loving gift for myself. (Choices for each are found on p. 13)

Physical_____

Intellectual_____

Emotional _____

Spiritual_____

☾Evening time pondering

What can I look forward to tomorrow?_____

5 things I am thankful for today_____

_____

_____

Sleep revitalizes me. I will prepare for sleep by_____
((Choices for preparation of sleep are on p. 17)

The Power of Self Care/Self Love: A Journal Workbook Into Your Higher Self

Good things are happening.

Today is ___/___/___

In this moment I feel_____

I affirm that I am_____
(Choices of affirmations are on p. 9)

Where can I create joy today?_____
(Choices of joys are on p.11)

I am a House with Four Rooms. I will open and air out each room as a caring and loving gift for myself. (Choices for each are found on p. 13)

Physical_____

Intellectual_____

Emotional _____

Spiritual_____

☾Evening time pondering

What can I look forward to tomorrow?_____

5 things I am thankful for today_____

_____

_____

Sleep revitalizes me. I will prepare for sleep by_____
((Choices for preparation of sleep are on p. 17)

The Power of Self Care/Self Love: A Journal Workbook Into Your Higher Self

Bloom where you are planted.
-St. Francis de Sales

Today is ___/___/___

In this moment I feel_____

I affirm that I am_____
(Choices of affirmations are on p. 9)

Where can I create joy today?_____
(Choices of joys are on p.11)

I am a House with Four Rooms. I will open and air out each room as a caring and loving gift for myself. (Choices for each are found on p. 13)

Physical_____

Intellectual_____

Emotional _____

Spiritual_____

☾Evening time pondering

What can I look forward to tomorrow?_____

5 things I am thankful for today_____
_____
_____

Sleep revitalizes me. I will prepare for sleep by_____
((Choices for preparation of sleep are on p. 17)

Change the way you look at things and the things you look at change.
-Dr. Wayne Dyer

Today is a new day. What if the things you feel are difficult or impossible are not that way at all? Write down the possibilities.

_____

_____

_____

_____

_____

_____

_____

_____

_____

_____

_____

The Power of Self Care/Self Love: A Journal Workbook Into Your Higher Self

The comfort zone is the great enemy to creativity; moving beyond it necessitates intuition, which in turn configures new perspectives and conquers fears. -Dan Stevens

Today is ___/___/___

In this moment I feel_____

I affirm that I am_____
(Choices of affirmations are on p. 9)

Where can I create joy today?_____
(Choices of joys are on p.11)

I am a House with Four Rooms. I will open and air out each room as a caring and loving gift for myself. (Choices for each are found on p. 13)

Physical_____

Intellectual_____

Emotional _____

Spiritual_____

☾Evening time pondering

What can I look forward to tomorrow?_____

5 things I am thankful for today_____

_____

_____

Sleep revitalizes me. I will prepare for sleep by_____
((Choices for preparation of sleep are on p. 17)

The Power of Self Care/Self Love: A Journal Workbook Into Your Higher Self

May my eyes be open today, that they might penetrate the darkness of a world that has forgotten love.
-Marianne Williamson

Today is ___/___/___

In this moment I feel_____

I affirm that I am_____
(Choices of affirmations are on p. 9)

Where can I create joy today?_____
(Choices of joys are on p.11)

I am a House with Four Rooms. I will open and air out each room as a caring and loving gift for myself. (Choices for each are found on p. 13)

Physical_____

Intellectual_____

Emotional _____

Spiritual_____

☾Evening time pondering

What can I look forward to tomorrow?_____

5 things I am thankful for today_____

_____

_____

Sleep revitalizes me. I will prepare for sleep by_____
((Choices for preparation of sleep are on p. 17)

The Power of Self Care/Self Love: A Journal Workbook Into Your Higher Self

We are never more than one grateful thought away from peace of heart.
-Brother David Steindl-Rast

Today is ___/___/___

In this moment I feel_____

I affirm that I am_____
(Choices of affirmations are on p. 9)

Where can I create joy today?_____
(Choices of joys are on p.11)

I am a House with Four Rooms. I will open and air out each room as a caring and loving gift for myself. (Choices for each are found on p. 13)

Physical_____

Intellectual_____

Emotional _____

Spiritual_____

☾Evening time pondering

What can I look forward to tomorrow?_____

5 things I am thankful for today_____

_____

_____

Sleep revitalizes me. I will prepare for sleep by_____
((Choices for preparation of sleep are on p. 17)

What Do You Need?

The Power of Self Care/Self Love: A Journal Workbook Into Your Higher Self

When you remember that you are Divine everything changes.

Today is ___/___/___

In this moment I feel_____

I affirm that I am_____
(Choices of affirmations are on p. 9)

Where can I create joy today?_____
(Choices of joys are on p.11)

I am a House with Four Rooms. I will open and air out each room as a caring and loving gift for myself. (Choices for each are found on p. 13)

Physical_____

Intellectual_____

Emotional _____

Spiritual_____

🌙 Evening time pondering

What can I look forward to tomorrow?_____

5 things I am thankful for today_____

_____

_____

Sleep revitalizes me. I will prepare for sleep by_____
((Choices for preparation of sleep are on p. 17)

The Power of Self Care/Self Love: A Journal Workbook Into Your Higher Self

If we wait until we're ready we'll be waiting
for the rest of our lives.
-Lemony Snicket

Today is ___/___/___

In this moment I feel_____

I affirm that I am_____
(Choices of affirmations are on p. 9)

Where can I create joy today?_____
(Choices of joys are on p.11)

I am a House with Four Rooms. I will open and air out each room as a caring and loving gift for myself. (Choices for each are found on p. 13)

Physical_____

Intellectual_____

Emotional _____

Spiritual_____

☾Evening time pondering

What can I look forward to tomorrow?_____

5 things I am thankful for today_____

_____

_____

Sleep revitalizes me. I will prepare for sleep by_____
((Choices for preparation of sleep are on p. 17)

Peace begins with a smile. -Mother Teresa

The simplicity of cultivating peace is easier than we think. What could you do to bring more peace into your life?

_____
_____
_____
_____
_____
_____
_____
_____
_____
_____
_____
_____
_____

The Power of Self Care/Self Love: A Journal Workbook Into Your Higher Self

*There is no such thing as failure.
Not trying may come close though.*

Today is ___/___/___

In this moment I feel_____

I affirm that I am_____
(Choices of affirmations are on p. 9)

Where can I create joy today?_____
(Choices of joys are on p.11)

I am a House with Four Rooms. I will open and air out each room as a caring and loving gift for myself. (Choices for each are found on p. 13)

Physical_____

Intellectual_____

Emotional _____

Spiritual_____

☾Evening time pondering

What can I look forward to tomorrow?_____

5 things I am thankful for today_____

_____

_____

Sleep revitalizes me. I will prepare for sleep by_____
((Choices for preparation of sleep are on p. 17)

The Power of Self Care/Self Love: A Journal Workbook Into Your Higher Self

The Power of Self Care/Self Love: A Journal Workbook Into Your Higher Self

Love creates new form, changes matter, and holds the cosmos together beyond time and space. It's in every one of us. It's what God is. -Dr. Wayne Dyer

Today is ___/___/___

In this moment I feel_____

I affirm that I am_____
(Choices of affirmations are on p. 9)

Where can I create joy today?_____
(Choices of joys are on p.11)

I am a House with Four Rooms. I will open and air out each room as a caring and loving gift for myself. (Choices for each are found on p. 13)

Physical_____

Intellectual_____

Emotional _____

Spiritual_____

🌙Evening time pondering

What can I look forward to tomorrow?_____

5 things I am thankful for today_____

_____

_____

Sleep revitalizes me. I will prepare for sleep by_____
((Choices for preparation of sleep are on p. 17)

People aren't overcome by situations or outside forces. Defeat comes from within. -Banana Yoshimoto

Today is ___/___/___

In this moment I feel_____

I affirm that I am_____
(Choices of affirmations are on p. 9)

Where can I create joy today?_____
(Choices of joys are on p.11)

I am a House with Four Rooms. I will open and air out each room as a caring and loving gift for myself. (Choices for each are found on p. 13)

Physical_____

Intellectual_____

Emotional _____

Spiritual_____

☽Evening time pondering

What can I look forward to tomorrow?_____

5 things I am thankful for today_____

_____

_____

Sleep revitalizes me. I will prepare for sleep by_____
((Choices for preparation of sleep are on p. 17)

The Power of Self Care/Self Love: A Journal Workbook Into Your Higher Self

The best things in life are free.
-Coco Chanel

Today is ___/___/___

In this moment I feel_____

I affirm that I am_____
(Choices of affirmations are on p. 9)

Where can I create joy today?_____
(Choices of joys are on p.11)

I am a House with Four Rooms. I will open and air out each room as a caring and loving gift for myself. (Choices for each are found on p. 13)

Physical_____

Intellectual_____

Emotional _____

Spiritual_____

☾Evening time pondering

What can I look forward to tomorrow?_____

5 things I am thankful for today_____

_____

_____

Sleep revitalizes me. I will prepare for sleep by_____
((Choices for preparation of sleep are on p. 17)

The Power of Self Care/Self Love: A Journal Workbook Into Your Higher Self

I will not allow my life's light to be determined by the darkness around me. -Sojourner Truth

Today is ___/___/___

In this moment I feel_____

I affirm that I am_____
Choices of affirmations are on p. 6)

Where can I create joy today?_____
(Choices of joys are on p.11)

I am a House with Four Rooms. I will open and air out each room as a caring and loving gift for myself. (Choices for each are found on p. 13)

Physical_____

Intellectual_____

Emotional _____

Spiritual_____

☾Evening time pondering

What can I look forward to tomorrow?_____

5 things I am thankful for today_____

_____

_____

Sleep revitalizes me. I will prepare for sleep by_____
((Choices for preparation of sleep are on p. 17)

You had the power all along my dear.
-Glinda, the Good Witch

What qualities do you have? What gifts do you bring? What do you love to create?

The Power of Self Care/Self Love: A Journal Workbook Into Your Higher Self

If you judge people you have no time to love them.
-Mother Teresa

Today is ___/___/___

In this moment I feel_____

I affirm that I am_____
(Choices of affirmations are on p. 9)

Where can I create joy today?_____
(Choices of joys are on p.11)

I am a House with Four Rooms. I will open and air out each room as a caring and loving gift for myself. (Choices for each are found on p. 13)

Physical_____

Intellectual_____

Emotional _____

Spiritual_____

☾Evening time pondering

What can I look forward to tomorrow?_____

5 things I am thankful for today_____

_____

_____

Sleep revitalizes me. I will prepare for sleep by_____
((Choices for preparation of sleep are on p. 17)

The Power of Self Care/Self Love: A Journal Workbook Into Your Higher Self

To have fun, remember how to act like a three-year-old.

Today is ___/___/___

In this moment I feel_____

I affirm that I am_____
(Choices of affirmations are on p. 9)

Where can I create joy today?_____
(Choices of joys are on p.11)

I am a House with Four Rooms. I will open and air out each room as a caring and loving gift for myself. (Choices for each are found on p. 13)

Physical_____

Intellectual_____

Emotional _____

Spiritual_____

☾Evening time pondering

What can I look forward to tomorrow?_____

5 things I am thankful for today_____

_____

_____

Sleep revitalizes me. I will prepare for sleep by_____
((Choices for preparation of sleep are on p. 17)

Mistakes are a fact of life. It is the response to the errors that count. -Nikki Giovanni

Today is ___/___/___

In this moment I feel_____

I affirm that I am_____
(Choices of affirmations are on p. 9)

Where can I create joy today?_____
(Choices of joys are on p.11)

I am a House with Four Rooms. I will open and air out each room as a caring and loving gift for myself. (Choices for each are found on p. 13)

Physical_____

Intellectual_____

Emotional _____

Spiritual_____

☽Evening time pondering

What can I look forward to tomorrow?_____

5 things I am thankful for today_____

_____

_____

Sleep revitalizes me. I will prepare for sleep by_____
((Choices for preparation of sleep are on p. 17)

The Power of Self Care/Self Love: A Journal Workbook Into Your Higher Self

"You have peace," the old woman said, "when you make it with yourself." -Mitch Albom

Today is ___/___/___

In this moment I feel_____

I affirm that I am_____
Choices of affirmations are on p. 6)

Where can I create joy today?_____
(Choices of joys are on p.11)

I am a House with Four Rooms. I will open and air out each room as a caring and loving gift for myself. (Choices for each are found on p. 13)

Physical_____

Intellectual_____

Emotional _____

Spiritual_____

☾Evening time pondering

What can I look forward to tomorrow?_____

5 things I am thankful for today_____
_____
_____

Sleep revitalizes me. I will prepare for sleep by_____
((Choices for preparation of sleep are on p. 17)

What Do You Need?

The Power of Self Care/Self Love: A Journal Workbook Into Your Higher Self

The past has no power over the present moment.
-Eckhart Tolle

Today is ___/___/___

In this moment I feel_____

I affirm that I am_____
(Choices of affirmations are on p. 9)

Where can I create joy today?_____
(Choices of joys are on p.11)

I am a House with Four Rooms. I will open and air out each room as a caring and loving gift for myself. (Choices for each are found on p. 13)

Physical_____

Intellectual_____

Emotional _____

Spiritual_____

🌙Evening time pondering

What can I look forward to tomorrow?_____

5 things I am thankful for today_____

_____

_____

Sleep revitalizes me. I will prepare for sleep by_____
((Choices for preparation of sleep are on p. 17)

No medicine cures what happiness cannot.
-Gabriel Garcia Marquez

What makes you happy? List them all here until you fill the page.

_____
_____
_____
_____
_____
_____
_____
_____
_____
_____
_____
_____
_____
_____

The Power of Self Care/Self Love: A Journal Workbook Into Your Higher Self

If we think we are spiritual beings with an infinite abundance of love and power to bring to the world, then we tend to behave that way. -Marianne Williamson

Today is ___/___/___

In this moment I feel_____

I affirm that I am_____
(Choices of affirmations are on p. 9)

Where can I create joy today?_____
(Choices of joys are on p.11)

I am a House with Four Rooms. I will open and air out each room as a caring and loving gift for myself. (Choices for each are found on p. 13)

Physical_____

Intellectual_____

Emotional _____

Spiritual_____

☾Evening time pondering

What can I look forward to tomorrow?_____

5 things I am thankful for today_____

_____

_____

Sleep revitalizes me. I will prepare for sleep by_____
((Choices for preparation of sleep are on p. 17)

I release any fears, judgements, or blockages that prevent me from speaking the truth of my feelings. -Catherine Pray

Today is ___/___/___

In this moment I feel_____

I affirm that I am_____
(Choices of affirmations are on p. 9)

Where can I create joy today?_____
(Choices of joys are on p.11)

I am a House with Four Rooms. I will open and air out each room as a caring and loving gift for myself. (Choices for each are found on p. 13)

Physical_____

Intellectual_____

Emotional _____

Spiritual_____

🌙 Evening time pondering

What can I look forward to tomorrow?_____

5 things I am thankful for today_____

_____

_____

Sleep revitalizes me. I will prepare for sleep by_____
((Choices for preparation of sleep are on p. 17)

The Power of Self Care/Self Love: A Journal Workbook Into Your Higher Self

I have made my world and it is a much better world than I ever saw outside. -Louise Nevelson

Today is ___/___/___

In this moment I feel_____

I affirm that I am_____
(Choices of affirmations are on p. 9)

Where can I create joy today?_____
(Choices of joys are on p.11)

I am a House with Four Rooms. I will open and air out each room as a caring and loving gift for myself. (Choices for each are found on p. 13)

Physical_____

Intellectual_____

Emotional _____

Spiritual_____

🌙 Evening time pondering

What can I look forward to tomorrow?_____

5 things I am thankful for today_____

_____

_____

Sleep revitalizes me. I will prepare for sleep by_____
((Choices for preparation of sleep are on p. 17)

The Power of Self Care/Self Love: A Journal Workbook Into Your Higher Self

Gratitude unlocks the fullness of life. It turns what we have into enough, and ...turns denial into acceptance, chaos to order, confusion to clarity. It can turn a meal into a feast. A house into a home. A stranger into a friend. -Melodie Beattie

Today is ___/___/___

In this moment I feel_____

I affirm that I am_____
(Choices of affirmations are on p. 9)

Where can I create joy today?_____
(Choices of joys are on p.11)

I am a House with Four Rooms. I will open and air out each room as a caring and loving gift for myself. (Choices for each are found on p. 13)

Physical_____

Intellectual_____

Emotional _____

Spiritual_____

🌙Evening time pondering

What can I look forward to tomorrow?_____

5 things I am thankful for today_____

_____

_____

Sleep revitalizes me. I will prepare for sleep by_____
((Choices for preparation of sleep are on p. 17)

The Power of Self Care/Self Love: A Journal Workbook Into Your Higher Self

No matter where we live on the planet or how difficult our situation seems to be, we have the ability to overcome and transcend our circumstances. -Louise Hay

Today is ___/___/___

In this moment I feel_____

I affirm that I am_____
(Choices of affirmations are on p. 9)

Where can I create joy today?_____
(Choices of joys are on p.11)

I am a House with Four Rooms. I will open and air out each room as a caring and loving gift for myself. (Choices for each are found on p. 13)

Physical_____

Intellectual_____

Emotional _____

Spiritual_____

☾Evening time pondering

What can I look forward to tomorrow?_____

5 things I am thankful for today_____

_____

_____

Sleep revitalizes me. I will prepare for sleep by_____
((Choices for preparation of sleep are on p. 17)

The Power of Self Care/Self Love: A Journal Workbook Into Your Higher Self

The love of self triggers our own evolution.

Today is ___/___/___

In this moment I feel_____

I affirm that I am_____
(Choices of affirmations are on p. 9)

Where can I create joy today?_____
(Choices of joys are on p.11)

I am a House with Four Rooms. I will open and air out each room as a caring and loving gift for myself. (Choices for each are found on p. 13)

Physical_____

Intellectual_____

Emotional_____

Spiritual_____

☾Evening time pondering

What can I look forward to tomorrow?_____

5 things I am thankful for today_____

_____

_____

Sleep revitalizes me. I will prepare for sleep by_____
((Choices for preparation of sleep are on p. 17)

Love yourself first and everything else falls into line. You really must love yourself to get anything done in this world. -Lucille Ball

How can you love yourself more? List the ways here until you fill the page.

_____
_____
_____
_____
_____
_____
_____
_____
_____
_____
_____
_____
_____

Life is either a daring adventure or nothing. To keep our faces toward change and behave like free spirits in the presence of fate is strength undefeatable. -Helen Keller

Today is ___/___/___

In this moment I feel_____

I affirm that I am_____
(Choices of affirmations are on p. 9)

Where can I create joy today?_____
(Choices of joys are on p.11)

I am a House with Four Rooms. I will open and air out each room as a caring and loving gift for myself. (Choices for each are found on p. 13)

Physical_____

Intellectual_____

Emotional _____

Spiritual_____

🌙 Evening time pondering

What can I look forward to tomorrow?_____

5 things I am thankful for today_____
_____
_____

Sleep revitalizes me. I will prepare for sleep by_____
((Choices for preparation of sleep are on p. 17)

The Power of Self Care/Self Love: A Journal Workbook Into Your Higher Self

Forever is composed of nows. -Emily Dickenson

Today is ___/___/___

In this moment I feel_____

I affirm that I am_____
(Choices of affirmations are on p. 9)

Where can I create joy today?_____
(Choices of joys are on p.11)

I am a House with Four Rooms. I will open and air out each room as a caring and loving gift for myself. (Choices for each are found on p. 13)

Physical_____

Intellectual_____

Emotional _____

Spiritual_____

☾Evening time pondering

What can I look forward to tomorrow?_____

5 things I am thankful for today_____

_____

_____

Sleep revitalizes me. I will prepare for sleep by_____
((Choices for preparation of sleep are on p. 17)

The Power of Self Care/Self Love: A Journal Workbook Into Your Higher Self

You can do this. -Coffee

Today is ___/___/___

In this moment I feel_____

I affirm that I am_____
(Choices of affirmations are on p. 9)

Where can I create joy today?_____
(Choices of joys are on p.11)

I am a House with Four Rooms. I will open and air out each room as a caring and loving gift for myself. (Choices for each are found on p. 13)

Physical_____

Intellectual_____

Emotional _____

Spiritual_____

🌙Evening time pondering

What can I look forward to tomorrow?_____

5 things I am thankful for today_____

_____

_____

Sleep revitalizes me. I will prepare for sleep by_____
((Choices for preparation of sleep are on p. 17)

The Power of Self Care/Self Love: A Journal Workbook Into Your Higher Self

Ours is not the task of fixing the entire world all at once, but of stretching out to mend the part of the world that is within our reach. -Clarisa Pinkola-Estes

Today is ___/___/___

In this moment I feel_____

I affirm that I am_____
(Choices of affirmations are on p. 9)

Where can I create joy today?_____
(Choices of joys are on p.11)

I am a House with Four Rooms. I will open and air out each room as a caring and loving gift for myself. (Choices for each are found on p. 13)

Physical_____

Intellectual_____

Emotional _____

Spiritual_____

☾Evening time pondering

What can I look forward to tomorrow?_____

5 things I am thankful for today_____

_____

_____

Sleep revitalizes me. I will prepare for sleep by_____
((Choices for preparation of sleep are on p. 17)

What Do You Need?

The Power of Self Care/Self Love: A Journal Workbook Into Your Higher Self

It isn't what we say or think that defines us, but what we do.
-Jane Austen

Today is ___/___/___

In this moment I feel_____

I affirm that I am_____
(Choices of affirmations are on p. 9)

Where can I create joy today?_____
(Choices of joys are on p.11)

I am a House with Four Rooms. I will open and air out each room as a caring and loving gift for myself. (Choices for each are found on p. 13)

Physical_____

Intellectual_____

Emotional _____

Spiritual_____

☾Evening time pondering

What can I look forward to tomorrow?_____

5 things I am thankful for today_____

_____

_____

Sleep revitalizes me. I will prepare for sleep by_____
((Choices for preparation of sleep are on p. 17)

The Power of Self Care/Self Love: A Journal Workbook Into Your Higher Self

The awareness of your brilliance awakens the stars.

Today is ___/___/___

In this moment I feel_____

I affirm that I am_____
(Choices of affirmations are on p. 9)

Where can I create joy today?_____
(Choices of joys are on p.11)

I am a House with Four Rooms. I will open and air out each room as a caring and loving gift for myself. (Choices for each are found on p. 13)

Physical_____

Intellectual_____

Emotional _____

Spiritual_____

☾Evening time pondering

What can I look forward to tomorrow?_____

5 things I am thankful for today_____

_____

_____

Sleep revitalizes me. I will prepare for sleep by_____
((Choices for preparation of sleep are on p. 17)

Resentment, anger, hatred are poisons that you drink, and you expect somebody else to die. life does not work like that. -Sadguru

Who are you angry at? Who do you hate? What would your life be like if you no longer felt this way?

_____

_____

_____

_____

_____

_____

_____

_____

_____

_____

The Power of Self Care/Self Love: A Journal Workbook Into Your Higher Self

Your dreams in life will have deeper meaning when they are tied to the greater good. -Tererai Trent

Today is ___/___/___

In this moment I feel_____

I affirm that I am_____
(Choices of affirmations are on p. 9)

Where can I create joy today?_____
(Choices of joys are on p.11)

I am a House with Four Rooms. I will open and air out each room as a caring and loving gift for myself. (Choices for each are found on p. 13)

Physical_____

Intellectual_____

Emotional _____

Spiritual_____

☾Evening time pondering

What can I look forward to tomorrow?_____

5 things I am thankful for today_____

_____

_____

Sleep revitalizes me. I will prepare for sleep by_____
((Choices for preparation of sleep are on p. 17)

The Power of Self Care/Self Love: A Journal Workbook Into Your Higher Self

Do not underestimate the effects of your pessimistic...friends. If someone is not making you stronger, they are making you weaker. -Tim Ferris

Today is ___/___/___

In this moment I feel_____

I affirm that I am_____
(Choices of affirmations are on p. 9)

Where can I create joy today?_____
(Choices of joys are on p.11)

I am a House with Four Rooms. I will open and air out each room as a caring and loving gift for myself. (Choices for each are found on p. 13)

Physical_____

Intellectual_____

Emotional _____

Spiritual_____

🌙Evening time pondering

What can I look forward to tomorrow?_____

5 things I am thankful for today_____

_____

_____

Sleep revitalizes me. I will prepare for sleep by_____
((Choices for preparation of sleep are on p. 17)

The Power of Self Care/Self Love: A Journal Workbook Into Your Higher Self

Inner peace is a deep breath.

Today is ___/___/___

In this moment I feel_____

I affirm that I am_____
(Choices of affirmations are on p. 9)

Where can I create joy today?_____
(Choices of joys are on p.11)

I am a House with Four Rooms. I will open and air out each room as a caring and loving gift for myself. (Choices for each are found on p. 13)

Physical_____

Intellectual_____

Emotional _____

Spiritual_____

☾Evening time pondering

What can I look forward to tomorrow?_____

5 things I am thankful for today_____

_____

_____

Sleep revitalizes me. I will prepare for sleep by_____
((Choices for preparation of sleep are on p. 17)

The Power of Self Care/Self Love: A Journal Workbook Into Your Higher Self

As a doctor, let me tell you what self-love does: Improves...hearing, eyesight, lowers blood pressure, increases pulmonary function and cardiac output….if we had a(n) epidemic of self-love...healthcare costs would go down dramatically... This is hard core science.
-Dr. Christiane Northrup

Today is ___/___/___

In this moment I feel_____

I affirm that I am_____
(Choices of affirmations are on p. 9)

Where can I create joy today?_____
(Choices of joys are on p.11)

I am a House with Four Rooms. I will open and air out each room as a caring and loving gift for myself. (Choices for each are found on p. 13)

Physical_____

Intellectual_____

Emotional _____

Spiritual_____

🌙Evening time pondering

What can I look forward to tomorrow?_____

5 things I am thankful for today_____

_____

_____

Sleep revitalizes me. I will prepare for sleep by_____
((Choices for preparation of sleep are on p. 17)

The Power of Self Care/Self Love: A Journal Workbook Into Your Higher Self

There are three ways to ultimate success: The first way is to be kind. The second way is to be kind. The third way is to be kind.
-Mr. Rogers

Today is ___/___/___

In this moment I feel_____

I affirm that I am_____
(Choices of affirmations are on p. 9)

Where can I create joy today?_____
(Choices of joys are on p.11)

I am a House with Four Rooms. I will open and air out each room as a caring and loving gift for myself. (Choices for each are found on p. 13)

Physical_____

Intellectual_____

Emotional _____

Spiritual_____

☾Evening time pondering

What can I look forward to tomorrow?_____

5 things I am thankful for today_____

_____

_____

Sleep revitalizes me. I will prepare for sleep by_____
((Choices for preparation of sleep are on p. 17)

The Power of Self Care/Self Love: A Journal Workbook Into Your Higher Self

Life is like a movie. Write your own ending. -Kermit the Frog

Today is ___/___/___

In this moment I feel_____

I affirm that I am_____
(Choices of affirmations are on p. 9)

Where can I create joy today?_____
(Choices of joys are on p.11)

I am a House with Four Rooms. I will open and air out each room as a caring and loving gift for myself. (Choices for each are found on p. 13)

Physical_____

Intellectual_____

Emotional _____

Spiritual_____

☾Evening time pondering

What can I look forward to tomorrow?_____

5 things I am thankful for today_____

_____

_____

Sleep revitalizes me. I will prepare for sleep by_____
((Choices for preparation of sleep are on p. 17)

Once you start believing that something is possible, you start to let it into your awareness and it starts to become true to you.
-Anita Moorjani

What do you need to believe in? List those things on this page. What steps can you take to make them possible?

_____

_____

_____

_____

_____

_____

_____

_____

_____

_____

_____

_____

_____

When our stress levels drop, biological resources are freed up for cell repair, immunity, and other beneficial functions.
-Dr. Dawson Church

Today is ___/___/___

In this moment I feel_____

I affirm that I am_____
(Choices of affirmations are on p. 9)

Where can I create joy today?_____
(Choices of joys are on p.11)

I am a House with Four Rooms. I will open and air out each room as a caring and loving gift for myself. (Choices for each are found on p. 13)

Physical_____

Intellectual_____

Emotional _____

Spiritual_____

🌙Evening time pondering

What can I look forward to tomorrow?_____

5 things I am thankful for today_____

_____

_____

Sleep revitalizes me. I will prepare for sleep by_____
((Choices for preparation of sleep are on p. 17)

The Power of Self Care/Self Love: A Journal Workbook Into Your Higher Self

The true measure of any society can be found in how it treats its most vulnerable members. -Mahatma Gandhi

Today is ___/___/___

In this moment I feel_____

I affirm that I am_____
(Choices of affirmations are on p. 9)

Where can I create joy today?_____
(Choices of joys are on p.11)

I am a House with Four Rooms. I will open and air out each room as a caring and loving gift for myself. (Choices for each are found on p. 13)

Physical_____

Intellectual_____

Emotional _____

Spiritual_____

☾Evening time pondering

What can I look forward to tomorrow?_____

5 things I am thankful for today_____

_____

_____

Sleep revitalizes me. I will prepare for sleep by_____
((Choices for preparation of sleep are on p. 17)

The Power of Self Care/Self Love: A Journal Workbook Into Your Higher Self

Our aspirations are our possibilities. -Samuel Johnson

Today is ___/___/___

In this moment I feel_____

I affirm that I am_____
(Choices of affirmations are on p. 9)

Where can I create joy today?_____
(Choices of joys are on p.11)

I am a House with Four Rooms. I will open and air out each room as a caring and loving gift for myself. (Choices for each are found on p. 13)

Physical_____

Intellectual_____

Emotional _____

Spiritual_____

☾Evening time pondering

What can I look forward to tomorrow?_____

5 things I am thankful for today_____

_____

_____

Sleep revitalizes me. I will prepare for sleep by_____
((Choices for preparation of sleep are on p. 17)

The Power of Self Care/Self Love: A Journal Workbook Into Your Higher Self

Our beliefs control our bodies, our minds, and thus our lives
-Dr. Bruce Lipton

Today is ___/___/___

In this moment I feel_____

I affirm that I am_____
(Choices of affirmations are on p. 9)

Where can I create joy today?_____
(Choices of joys are on p.11)

I am a House with Four Rooms. I will open and air out each room as a caring and loving gift for myself. (Choices for each are found on p. 13)

Physical_____

Intellectual_____

Emotional _____

Spiritual_____

🌙 Evening time pondering

What can I look forward to tomorrow?_____

5 things I am thankful for today_____

_____

_____

Sleep revitalizes me. I will prepare for sleep by_____
((Choices for preparation of sleep are on p. 17)

What Do You Need?

The Power of Self Care/Self Love: A Journal Workbook Into Your Higher Self

The Power of Self Care/Self Love: A Journal Workbook Into Your Higher Self

You only live once, but if you do it right, once is enough.
-Mae West

Today is ___/___/___

In this moment I feel_____

I affirm that I am_____
(Choices of affirmations are on p. 9)

Where can I create joy today?_____
(Choices of joys are on p.11)

I am a House with Four Rooms. I will open and air out each room as a caring and loving gift for myself. (Choices for each are found on p. 13)

Physical_____

Intellectual_____

Emotional _____

Spiritual_____

🌙Evening time pondering

What can I look forward to tomorrow?_____

5 things I am thankful for today_____
_____
_____

Sleep revitalizes me. I will prepare for sleep by_____
((Choices for preparation of sleep are on p. 17)

***The more that you read, the more things you will know.
The more that you learn, the more places you will go.***
-Dr. Seuss

What topics interest you? What books or audiobooks can you order on those topics? Do you know anyone who can recommend enjoyable books?

The Power of Self Care/Self Love: A Journal Workbook Into Your Higher Self

You are so full of hatred, you will never be a true king
-Okoye, Black Panther

Today is ___/___/___

In this moment I feel_____

I affirm that I am_____
(Choices of affirmations are on p. 9)

Where can I create joy today?_____
(Choices of joys are on p.11)

I am a House with Four Rooms. I will open and air out each room as a caring and loving gift for myself. (Choices for each are found on p. 13)

Physical_____

Intellectual_____

Emotional _____

Spiritual_____

🌙Evening time pondering

What can I look forward to tomorrow?_____

5 things I am thankful for today_____

_____

_____

Sleep revitalizes me. I will prepare for sleep by_____
((Choices for preparation of sleep are on p. 17)

The Power of Self Care/Self Love: A Journal Workbook Into Your Higher Self

Today I declare full responsibility for my life. I see beautiful results in everything I do. I achieve everything I imagine and desire for my life. -Catherine Pray

Today is ___/___/___

In this moment I feel_____

I affirm that I am_____
(Choices of affirmations are on p. 9)

Where can I create joy today?_____
(Choices of joys are on p.11)

I am a House with Four Rooms. I will open and air out each room as a caring and loving gift for myself. (Choices for each are found on p. 13)

Physical_____

Intellectual_____

Emotional _____

Spiritual_____

☾Evening time pondering

What can I look forward to tomorrow?_____

5 things I am thankful for today_____

_____

_____

Sleep revitalizes me. I will prepare for sleep by_____
((Choices for preparation of sleep are on p. 17)

The Power of Self Care/Self Love: A Journal Workbook Into Your Higher Self

Holding someone's hand creates a flow of energy that cannot be broken.

Today is ___/___/___

In this moment I feel_____

I affirm that I am_____
(Choices of affirmations are on p. 9)

Where can I create joy today?_____
(Choices of joys are on p.11)

I am a House with Four Rooms. I will open and air out each room as a caring and loving gift for myself. (Choices for each are found on p. 13)

Physical_____

Intellectual_____

Emotional _____

Spiritual_____

☾Evening time pondering

What can I look forward to tomorrow?_____

5 things I am thankful for today_____

_____

_____

Sleep revitalizes me. I will prepare for sleep by_____
((Choices for preparation of sleep are on p. 17)

The Power of Self Care/Self Love: A Journal Workbook Into Your Higher Self

As I began to love myself, I freed myself of anything...not good for my health-food, people, things, situations, and everything that drew me down and away from myself. At first, I called this attitude a healthy egoism. Today I know it is love for oneself. -Charlie Chaplin

Today is ___/___/___

In this moment I feel_____

I affirm that I am_____
(Choices of affirmations are on p. 9)

Where can I create joy today?_____
(Choices of joys are on p.11)

I am a House with Four Rooms. I will open and air out each room as a caring and loving gift for myself. (Choices for each are found on p. 13)

Physical_____

Intellectual_____

Emotional _____

Spiritual_____

☾Evening time pondering

What can I look forward to tomorrow?_____

5 things I am thankful for today_____
_____
_____

Sleep revitalizes me. I will prepare for sleep by_____
((Choices for preparation of sleep are on p. 17)

The Power of Self Care/Self Love: A Journal Workbook Into Your Higher Self

Love is where you least expect it, so look there first. -Miss Piggy

Today is ___/___/___

In this moment I feel_____

I affirm that I am_____
(Choices of affirmations are on p. 9)

Where can I create joy today?_____
(Choices of joys are on p.11)

I am a House with Four Rooms. I will open and air out each room as a caring and loving gift for myself. (Choices for each are found on p. 13)

Physical_____

Intellectual_____

Emotional _____

Spiritual_____

🌙Evening time pondering

What can I look forward to tomorrow?_____

5 things I am thankful for today_____

_____

_____

Sleep revitalizes me. I will prepare for sleep by_____
((Choices for preparation of sleep are on p. 17)

The Power of Self Care/Self Love: A Journal Workbook Into Your Higher Self

Darkness cannot drive out darkness: Only light can do that. Hate cannot drive out hate: Only love can do that.
-Dr. Martin Luther King, Jr.

Today is ___/___/___

In this moment I feel_____

I affirm that I am_____
(Choices of affirmations are on p. 9)

Where can I create joy today?_____
(Choices of joys are on p.11)

I am a House with Four Rooms. I will open and air out each room as a caring and loving gift for myself. (Choices for each are found on p. 13)

Physical_____

Intellectual_____

Emotional _____

Spiritual_____

☾Evening time pondering

What can I look forward to tomorrow?_____

5 things I am thankful for today_____

_____

_____

Sleep revitalizes me. I will prepare for sleep by_____
((Choices for preparation of sleep are on p. 17)

Do not look for joy anywhere else. It is living in you and gives meaning to all existence.
-Judith Hanson Lasater

What if you created joy for yourself? What if you stopped blaming others for your joylessness? Write on this page the simple things you create that bring you joy.

_____

_____

_____

_____

_____

_____

_____

_____

_____

_____

The Power of Self Care/Self Love: A Journal Workbook Into Your Higher Self

A human being is a part of the...universe...He experiences himself...as...separated from the rest, an optical delusion of his consciousness. This delusion ....restricts us to our personal desires and to affection for a few persons nearest to us. Our task must be to free ourselves...by widening our circle of compassion to embrace all living creatures.
-Albert Einstein

Today is ___/___/___

In this moment I feel_____

I affirm that I am_____
(Choices of affirmations are on p. 9)

Where can I create joy today?_____
(Choices of joys are on p.11)

I am a House with Four Rooms. I will open and air out each room as a caring and loving gift for myself. (Choices for each are found on p. 13)

Physical_____

Intellectual_____

Emotional _____

Spiritual_____

☾Evening time pondering

What can I look forward to tomorrow?_____

5 things I am thankful for today_____

_____

_____

Sleep revitalizes me. I will prepare for sleep by_____
((Choices for preparation of sleep are on p. 17)

The Power of Self Care/Self Love: A Journal Workbook Into Your Higher Self

Change is brought about because ordinary people do extraordinary things. -Barack Obama

Today is ___/___/___

In this moment I feel_____

I affirm that I am_____
(Choices of affirmations are on p. 9)

Where can I create joy today?_____
(Choices of joys are on p.11)

I am a House with Four Rooms. I will open and air out each room as a caring and loving gift for myself. (Choices for each are found on p. 13)

Physical_____

Intellectual_____

Emotional _____

Spiritual_____

☾Evening time pondering

What can I look forward to tomorrow?_____

5 things I am thankful for today_____

_____

_____

Sleep revitalizes me. I will prepare for sleep by_____
((Choices for preparation of sleep are on p. 17)

276

Nothing is possible on this planet without courage. It is the most significant quality of a person out there. -Aristotle

Today is ___/___/___

In this moment I feel_____

I affirm that I am_____
(Choices of affirmations are on p. 9)

Where can I create joy today?_____
(Choices of joys are on p.11)

I am a House with Four Rooms. I will open and air out each room as a caring and loving gift for myself. (Choices for each are found on p. 13)

Physical_____

Intellectual_____

Emotional _____

Spiritual_____

☾Evening time pondering

What can I look forward to tomorrow?_____

5 things I am thankful for today_____

_____

_____

Sleep revitalizes me. I will prepare for sleep by_____
((Choices for preparation of sleep are on p. 17)

Success is not final, failure is not fatal: it is the courage to continue that counts. -Winston Churchill

Today is ___/___/___

In this moment I feel_____

I affirm that I am_____
(Choices of affirmations are on p. 9)

Where can I create joy today?_____
(Choices of joys are on p.11)

I am a House with Four Rooms. I will open and air out each room as a caring and loving gift for myself. (Choices for each are found on p. 13)

Physical_____

Intellectual_____

Emotional _____

Spiritual_____

☾Evening time pondering

What can I look forward to tomorrow?_____

5 things I am thankful for today_____
_____
_____

Sleep revitalizes me. I will prepare for sleep by_____
((Choices for preparation of sleep are on p. 17)

A good laugh and a long sleep are the two best cures for anything. -Irish Proverb

Today is ___/___/___

In this moment I feel_____

I affirm that I am_____
(Choices of affirmations are on p. 9)

Where can I create joy today?_____
(Choices of joys are on p.11)

I am a House with Four Rooms. I will open and air out each room as a caring and loving gift for myself. (Choices for each are found on p. 13)

Physical_____

Intellectual_____

Emotional _____

Spiritual_____

☾Evening time pondering

What can I look forward to tomorrow?_____

5 things I am thankful for today_____

_____

_____

Sleep revitalizes me. I will prepare for sleep by_____
((Choices for preparation of sleep are on p. 17)

What Do You Need?

Holding on to anger is like grasping a hot coal with the intent of throwing it at someone else; you are the one who gets burned.
-The Buddha

Today is ___/___/___

In this moment I feel_____

I affirm that I am_____
(Choices of affirmations are on p. 9)

Where can I create joy today?_____
(Choices of joys are on p.11)

I am a House with Four Rooms. I will open and air out each room as a caring and loving gift for myself. (Choices for each are found on p. 13)

Physical_____

Intellectual_____

Emotional _____

Spiritual_____

🌙Evening time pondering

What can I look forward to tomorrow?_____

5 things I am thankful for today_____

_____

_____

Sleep revitalizes me. I will prepare for sleep by_____
((Choices for preparation of sleep are on p. 17)

And the day came when the risk to remain tight in a bud was more painful than the risk it took to blossom.
-Anais Nin

Sometimes it takes more energy to remain the same then it does to evolve. Are you being called to do something different? What is your body saying? Write down what your heart needs.

_____

_____

_____

_____

_____

_____

_____

_____

_____

_____

_____

_____

_____

The Power of Self Care/Self Love: A Journal Workbook Into Your Higher Self

I learned that courage was not the absence of fear, but the triumph over it. -Nelson Mandela

Today is ___/___/___

In this moment I feel_____

I affirm that I am_____
(Choices of affirmations are on p. 9)

Where can I create joy today?_____
(Choices of joys are on p.11)

I am a House with Four Rooms. I will open and air out each room as a caring and loving gift for myself. (Choices for each are found on p. 13)

Physical_____

Intellectual_____

Emotional _____

Spiritual_____

🌙 Evening time pondering

What can I look forward to tomorrow?_____

5 things I am thankful for today_____

_____

_____

Sleep revitalizes me. I will prepare for sleep by_____
((Choices for preparation of sleep are on p. 17)

If you only do what you can do, you will never be more than you are now. -Jennifer Yuh Nelson

Today is ___/___/___

In this moment I feel_____

I affirm that I am_____
(Choices of affirmations are on p. 9)

Where can I create joy today?_____
(Choices of joys are on p.11)

I am a House with Four Rooms. I will open and air out each room as a caring and loving gift for myself. (Choices for each are found on p. 13)

Physical_____

Intellectual_____

Emotional _____

Spiritual_____

☾Evening time pondering

What can I look forward to tomorrow?_____

5 things I am thankful for today_____

_____

_____

Sleep revitalizes me. I will prepare for sleep by_____
((Choices for preparation of sleep are on p. 17)

People sometimes attribute my success to my genius; All the genius I know is hard work. -Alexander Hamilton

Today is ___/___/___

In this moment I feel_____

I affirm that I am_____
(Choices of affirmations are on p. 9)

Where can I create joy today?_____
(Choices of joys are on p.11)

I am a House with Four Rooms. I will open and air out each room as a caring and loving gift for myself. (Choices for each are found on p. 13)

Physical_____

Intellectual_____

Emotional _____

Spiritual_____

☾Evening time pondering

What can I look forward to tomorrow?_____

5 things I am thankful for today_____

_____

_____

Sleep revitalizes me. I will prepare for sleep by_____
((Choices for preparation of sleep are on p. 17)

The Power of Self Care/Self Love: A Journal Workbook Into Your Higher Self

Thankfully, perseverance is a good substitute for talent.
-Steve Martin

Today is ___/___/___

In this moment I feel_____

I affirm that I am_____
(Choices of affirmations are on p. 9)

Where can I create joy today?_____
(Choices of joys are on p.11)

I am a House with Four Rooms. I will open and air out each room as a caring and loving gift for myself. (Choices for each are found on p. 13)

Physical_____

Intellectual_____

Emotional _____

Spiritual_____

☽Evening time pondering

What can I look forward to tomorrow?_____

5 things I am thankful for today_____

_____

_____

Sleep revitalizes me. I will prepare for sleep by_____
((Choices for preparation of sleep are on p. 17)

The Power of Self Care/Self Love: A Journal Workbook Into Your Higher Self

It makes no difference as to the name of the God, since love is the real God of all the world. -Apache proverb

Today is ___/___/___

In this moment I feel_____

I affirm that I am_____
(Choices of affirmations are on p. 9)

Where can I create joy today?_____
(Choices of joys are on p.11)

I am a House with Four Rooms. I will open and air out each room as a caring and loving gift for myself. (Choices for each are found on p. 13)

Physical_____

Intellectual_____

Emotional _____

Spiritual_____

☾Evening time pondering

What can I look forward to tomorrow?_____

5 things I am thankful for today_____

_____

_____

Sleep revitalizes me. I will prepare for sleep by_____
((Choices for preparation of sleep are on p. 17)

I love my age. Old enough to know better. Young enough not to care. Experienced enough to do it right. -Angela Bassett

Today is ___/___/___

In this moment I feel_____

I affirm that I am_____
(Choices of affirmations are on p. 9)

Where can I create joy today?_____
(Choices of joys are on p.11)

I am a House with Four Rooms. I will open and air out each room as a caring and loving gift for myself. (Choices for each are found on p. 13)

Physical_____

Intellectual_____

Emotional _____

Spiritual_____

🌙Evening time pondering

What can I look forward to tomorrow?_____

5 things I am thankful for today_____

_____

_____

Sleep revitalizes me. I will prepare for sleep by_____
((Choices for preparation of sleep are on p. 17)

The Power of Self Care/Self Love: A Journal Workbook Into Your Higher Self

Little by little the bird makes its nest. -French proverb

What small steps can you take to care for and love yourself? What needs to change within you? What needs to be created?

_____
_____
_____
_____
_____
_____
_____
_____
_____
_____
_____
_____
_____
_____
_____

The Power of Self Care/Self Love: A Journal Workbook Into Your Higher Self

For beautiful eyes, look for the good in others; for beautiful lips, speak only words of kindness; and for poise, walk with the knowledge that you are never alone. -Audrey Hepburn

Today is ___/___/___

In this moment I feel_____

I affirm that I am_____
(Choices of affirmations are on p. 9)

Where can I create joy today?_____
(Choices of joys are on p.11)

I am a House with Four Rooms. I will open and air out each room as a caring and loving gift for myself. (Choices for each are found on p. 13)

Physical_____

Intellectual_____

Emotional _____

Spiritual_____

🌙Evening time pondering

What can I look forward to tomorrow?_____

5 things I am thankful for today_____

_____

_____

Sleep revitalizes me. I will prepare for sleep by_____
((Choices for preparation of sleep are on p. 17)

The Power of Self Care/Self Love: A Journal Workbook Into Your Higher Self

Today I will do what others won't, so tomorrow I can accomplish what others can't. -Jerry Rice

Today is ___/___/___

In this moment I feel_____

I affirm that I am_____
(Choices of affirmations are on p. 9)

Where can I create joy today?_____
(Choices of joys are on p.11)

I am a House with Four Rooms. I will open and air out each room as a caring and loving gift for myself. (Choices for each are found on p. 13)

Physical_____

Intellectual_____

Emotional _____

Spiritual_____

🌙 Evening time pondering

What can I look forward to tomorrow?_____

5 things I am thankful for today_____

_____

_____

Sleep revitalizes me. I will prepare for sleep by_____
((Choices for preparation of sleep are on p. 17)

The Power of Self Care/Self Love: A Journal Workbook Into Your Higher Self

I love walking in the woods, on the trails, along the beaches. I love being part of nature. I love being alone. It is therapy. One needs to be alone to recharge one's batteries. -Grace Kelly

Today is ___/___/___

In this moment I feel_____

I affirm that I am_____
(Choices of affirmations are on p. 9)

Where can I create joy today?_____
(Choices of joys are on p.11)

I am a House with Four Rooms. I will open and air out each room as a caring and loving gift for myself. (Choices for each are found on p. 13)

Physical_____

Intellectual_____

Emotional_____

Spiritual_____

🌙 Evening time pondering

What can I look forward to tomorrow?_____

5 things I am thankful for today_____

_____

_____

Sleep revitalizes me. I will prepare for sleep by_____
((Choices for preparation of sleep are on p. 17)

The Power of Self Care/Self Love: A Journal Workbook Into Your Higher Self

You do not need to know precisely what is happening, or …where it is all going…you need to recognize the possibilities and challenges offered by the present moment, and to embrace them with courage, faith, and hope. -Thomas Merton

Today is ___/___/___

In this moment I feel_____

I affirm that I am_____
(Choices of affirmations are on p. 9)

Where can I create joy today?_____
(Choices of joys are on p.11)

I am a House with Four Rooms. I will open and air out each room as a caring and loving gift for myself. (Choices for each are found on p. 13)

Physical_____

Intellectual_____

Emotional _____

Spiritual_____

☾Evening time pondering

What can I look forward to tomorrow?_____

5 things I am thankful for today_____

_____

_____

Sleep revitalizes me. I will prepare for sleep by_____
((Choices for preparation of sleep are on p. 17)

Vision Board #3
What I Want to Start

It has been 270 days and it's time to indulge yourself with your third creative vision board, What do you want to Start?

The sky's the limit here. Be creative. If there is a little voice in your head saying, "Don't be ridiculous", tell it to take a hike. Place a divine loving light in and around your empty board. Let go of fear. Allow your dreams to rest here.

Like a scavenger hunt, look for what you have cut out or printed and taped to the last 10 pages. If there is not much there then take some time today to explore magazines, newspapers, Pinterest, or Canva and cut out and print your items on an 11x14 (or larger) cork board, thick poster board, magnetic dry erase board, or canvas.

There are no rules, just a fun exploration of what your body, mind and spirit want to start.

Vision boards can have:
sticky notes
Colored paper sheets
3x5 index cards
A poem
Well-thought-out typed words
Pictures of what you love
Real pictures of you, family, friends

Remember this is a fun activity so grab your scissors, glue, scotch tape, markers, push pins or magnets.

What Do You Need?

The Power of Self Care/Self Love: A Journal Workbook Into Your Higher Self

Gratitude is riches. Complaint is poverty. -Doris Day

Today is ___/___/___

In this moment I feel_____

I affirm that I am_____
(Choices of affirmations are on p. 9)

Where can I create joy today?_____
(Choices of joys are on p.11)

I am a House with Four Rooms. I will open and air out each room as a caring and loving gift for myself. (Choices for each are found on p. 13)

Physical_____

Intellectual_____

Emotional _____

Spiritual_____

🌙Evening time pondering

What can I look forward to tomorrow?_____

5 things I am thankful for today_____

_____

_____

Sleep revitalizes me. I will prepare for sleep by_____
((Choices for preparation of sleep are on p. 17)

My son, the battle is between two wolves inside us all. One is evil, the other is good. The same fight is going on inside you. Which wolf wins grandfather?
The one you feed. -Cherokee elder

Is there a struggle within you? Can you write it down here?

_____

_____

_____

_____

_____

_____

_____

_____

_____

_____

_____

The Power of Self Care/Self Love: A Journal Workbook Into Your Higher Self

Obstacles don't have to stop you. If you run into a wall, don't turn around and give up. Figure out how to climb it, go through it or work around it. -Michael Jordan

Today is ___/___/___

In this moment I feel_____

I affirm that I am_____
(Choices of affirmations are on p. 9)

Where can I create joy today?_____
(Choices of joys are on p.11)

I am a House with Four Rooms. I will open and air out each room as a caring and loving gift for myself. (Choices for each are found on p. 13)

Physical_____

Intellectual_____

Emotional _____

Spiritual_____

☾Evening time pondering

What can I look forward to tomorrow?_____

5 things I am thankful for today_____

_____

_____

Sleep revitalizes me. I will prepare for sleep by_____
((Choices for preparation of sleep are on p. 17)

The Power of Self Care/Self Love: A Journal Workbook Into Your Higher Self

Very often you are in the right place, at the right time, you just don't know it. -Maria Tallchief

Today is ___/___/___

In this moment I feel_____

I affirm that I am_____
(Choices of affirmations are on p. 9)

Where can I create joy today?_____
(Choices of joys are on p.11)

I am a House with Four Rooms. I will open and air out each room as a caring and loving gift for myself. (Choices for each are found on p. 13)

Physical_____

Intellectual_____

Emotional _____

Spiritual_____

☾Evening time pondering

What can I look forward to tomorrow?_____

5 things I am thankful for today_____

_____

_____

Sleep revitalizes me. I will prepare for sleep by_____
((Choices for preparation of sleep are on p. 17)

The Power of Self Care/Self Love: A Journal Workbook Into Your Higher Self

Nobody can make the sound you make. -Yo-Yo Ma

Today is ___/___/___

In this moment I feel_____

I affirm that I am_____
(Choices of affirmations are on p. 9)

Where can I create joy today?_____
(Choices of joys are on p.11)

I am a House with Four Rooms. I will open and air out each room as a caring and loving gift for myself. (Choices for each are found on p. 13)

Physical_____

Intellectual_____

Emotional _____

Spiritual_____

🌙 Evening time pondering

What can I look forward to tomorrow?_____

5 things I am thankful for today_____

_____

_____

Sleep revitalizes me. I will prepare for sleep by_____
((Choices for preparation of sleep are on p. 17)

The Power of Self Care/Self Love: A Journal Workbook Into Your Higher Self

I firmly believe that in every situation, no matter how difficult, God extends grace greater than the hardship, and strength and peace of mind that can lead us to a place higher than where we were before. -Andy Griffith

Today is ___/___/___

In this moment I feel_____

I affirm that I am_____
(Choices of affirmations are on p. 9)

Where can I create joy today?_____
(Choices of joys are on p.11)

I am a House with Four Rooms. I will open and air out each room as a caring and loving gift for myself. (Choices for each are found on p. 13)

Physical_____

Intellectual_____

Emotional_____

Spiritual_____

☾Evening time pondering

What can I look forward to tomorrow?_____

5 things I am thankful for today_____

_____

_____

Sleep revitalizes me. I will prepare for sleep by_____
((Choices for preparation of sleep are on p. 17)

The Power of Self Care/Self Love: A Journal Workbook Into Your Higher Self

You must be doing something you enjoy. That is the definition of happiness. -Jackie Kennedy

Today is ___/___/___

In this moment I feel_____

I affirm that I am_____
(Choices of affirmations are on p. 9)

Where can I create joy today?_____
(Choices of joys are on p.11)

I am a House with Four Rooms. I will open and air out each room as a caring and loving gift for myself. (Choices for each are found on p. 13)

Physical_____

Intellectual_____

Emotional _____

Spiritual_____

☾Evening time pondering

What can I look forward to tomorrow?_____

5 things I am thankful for today_____

_____

_____

Sleep revitalizes me. I will prepare for sleep by_____
((Choices for preparation of sleep are on p. 17)

In the middle of chaos lies opportunity. -Bruce Lee

What if everything that is not going well right now is supposed to be occurring to help you grow? Can you see anything positive in the chaos that is happening?

The Power of Self Care/Self Love: A Journal Workbook Into Your Higher Self

Remember that when you leave this earth, you can take with you nothing that you have received - only what you have given: a full heart, enriched by honest service, love, sacrifice and courage. - St. Francis of Assisi

Today is ___/___/___

In this moment I feel_____

I affirm that I am_____
(Choices of affirmations are on p. 9)

Where can I create joy today?_____
(Choices of joys are on p.11)

I am a House with Four Rooms. I will open and air out each room as a caring and loving gift for myself. (Choices for each are found on p. 13)

Physical_____

Intellectual_____

Emotional _____

Spiritual_____

🌙Evening time pondering

What can I look forward to tomorrow?_____

5 things I am thankful for today_____

_____

_____

Sleep revitalizes me. I will prepare for sleep by_____
((Choices for preparation of sleep are on p. 17)

The Power of Self Care/Self Love: A Journal Workbook Into Your Higher Self

The Power of Self Care/Self Love: A Journal Workbook Into Your Higher Self

Seems to me, it ain't the world that's so bad but what we're doing to it. And all I'm saying is, see, what a wonderful world it would be if only we'd give it a chance. Love baby, love. That is the secret. -Louis Armstrong

Today is ___/___/___

In this moment I feel_____

I affirm that I am_____
(Choices of affirmations are on p. 9)

Where can I create joy today?_____
(Choices of joys are on p.11)

I am a House with Four Rooms. I will open and air out each room as a caring and loving gift for myself. (Choices for each are found on p. 13)

Physical_____

Intellectual_____

Emotional _____

Spiritual_____

☾Evening time pondering

What can I look forward to tomorrow?_____

5 things I am thankful for today_____

_____

_____

Sleep revitalizes me. I will prepare for sleep by_____
((Choices for preparation of sleep are on p. 17)

The Power of Self Care/Self Love: A Journal Workbook Into Your Higher Self

Every one of us needs to show how much we care for each other and, in the process, care for ourselves. -Princess Diana

Today is ___/___/___

In this moment I feel_____

I affirm that I am_____
(Choices of affirmations are on p. 9)

Where can I create joy today?_____
(Choices of joys are on p.11)

I am a House with Four Rooms. I will open and air out each room as a caring and loving gift for myself. (Choices for each are found on p. 13)

Physical_____

Intellectual_____

Emotional _____

Spiritual_____

☾ Evening time pondering

What can I look forward to tomorrow?_____

5 things I am thankful for today_____

_____

_____

Sleep revitalizes me. I will prepare for sleep by_____
((Choices for preparation of sleep are on p. 17)

The Power of Self Care/Self Love: A Journal Workbook Into Your Higher Self

The most powerful words in the universe are the words you say to yourself. -Marie Forleo

Today is ___/___/___

In this moment I feel_____

I affirm that I am_____
(Choices of affirmations are on p. 9)

Where can I create joy today?_____
(Choices of joys are on p.11)

I am a House with Four Rooms. I will open and air out each room as a caring and loving gift for myself. (Choices for each are found on p. 13)

Physical_____

Intellectual_____

Emotional _____

Spiritual_____

☾Evening time pondering

What can I look forward to tomorrow?_____

5 things I am thankful for today_____

_____

_____

Sleep revitalizes me. I will prepare for sleep by_____
((Choices for preparation of sleep are on p. 17)

Do not forget to tell your favorite people that you love them. -Shirley Temple

List all the people here that need to hear you say, "I love you." Start with saying it to yourself.

_____

_____

_____

_____

_____

_____

_____

_____

_____

_____

_____

_____

_____

The Power of Self Care/Self Love: A Journal Workbook Into Your Higher Self

The one lesson I have learned is that there is no substitute for paying attention. -Diane Sawyer

Today is ___/___/___

In this moment I feel_____

I affirm that I am_____
(Choices of affirmations are on p. 9)

Where can I create joy today?_____
(Choices of joys are on p.11)

I am a House with Four Rooms. I will open and air out each room as a caring and loving gift for myself. (Choices for each are found on p. 13)

Physical_____

Intellectual_____

Emotional _____

Spiritual_____

☾Evening time pondering

What can I look forward to tomorrow?_____

5 things I am thankful for today_____

_____

_____

Sleep revitalizes me. I will prepare for sleep by_____

What Do You Need?

The Power of Self Care/Self Love: A Journal Workbook Into Your Higher Self

I never said, 'I want to be alone.' I only said, 'I want to be left alone!' There is all the difference. -Greta Garbo

Today is ___/___/___

In this moment I feel_____

I affirm that I am_____
(Choices of affirmations are on p. 9)

Where can I create joy today?_____
(Choices of joys are on p.11)

I am a House with Four Rooms. I will open and air out each room as a caring and loving gift for myself. (Choices for each are found on p. 13)

Physical_____

Intellectual_____

Emotional _____

Spiritual_____

🌙Evening time pondering

What can I look forward to tomorrow?_____

5 things I am thankful for today_____

_____

_____

Sleep revitalizes me. I will prepare for sleep by_____
((Choices for preparation of sleep are on p. 17)

The Power of Self Care/Self Love: A Journal Workbook Into Your Higher Self

To face despair and not give into it, that's courage. -Ted Koppel

Today is ___/___/___

In this moment I feel_____

I affirm that I am_____
(Choices of affirmations are on p. 9)

Where can I create joy today?_____
(Choices of joys are on p.11)

I am a House with Four Rooms. I will open and air out each room as a caring and loving gift for myself. (Choices for each are found on p. 13)

Physical_____

Intellectual_____

Emotional _____

Spiritual_____

☾Evening time pondering

What can I look forward to tomorrow?_____

5 things I am thankful for today_____

_____

_____

Sleep revitalizes me. I will prepare for sleep by_____
((Choices for preparation of sleep are on p. 17)

The Power of Self Care/Self Love: A Journal Workbook Into Your Higher Self

It's hard to beat a person that never gives up. -Babe Ruth

Today is ___/___/___

In this moment I feel_____

I affirm that I am_____
(Choices of affirmations are on p. 9)

Where can I create joy today?_____
(Choices of joys are on p.11)

I am a House with Four Rooms. I will open and air out each room as a caring and loving gift for myself. (Choices for each are found on p. 13)

Physical_____

Intellectual_____

Emotional _____

Spiritual_____

☾Evening time pondering

What can I look forward to tomorrow?_____

5 things I am thankful for today_____

_____

_____

Sleep revitalizes me. I will prepare for sleep by_____
((Choices for preparation of sleep are on p. 17)

The Power of Self Care/Self Love: A Journal Workbook Into Your Higher Self

Humor is your own unconscious therapy. Like a welcome summer rain, humor may suddenly cleanse and cool the earth, the air, and you. -Langston Hughes

Today is ___/___/___

In this moment I feel_____

I affirm that I am_____
(Choices of affirmations are on p. 9)

Where can I create joy today?_____
(Choices of joys are on p.11)

I am a House with Four Rooms. I will open and air out each room as a caring and loving gift for myself. (Choices for each are found on p. 13)

Physical_____

Intellectual_____

Emotional _____

Spiritual_____

🌙Evening time pondering

What can I look forward to tomorrow?_____

5 things I am thankful for today_____

_____

_____

Sleep revitalizes me. I will prepare for sleep by_____
((Choices for preparation of sleep are on p. 17)

It is through art that we will prevail, and we will endure. It lives on after us and defines us as people. -Rita Moreno

Today is ___/___/___

In this moment I feel_____

I affirm that I am_____
(Choices of affirmations are on p. 9)

Where can I create joy today?_____
(Choices of joys are on p.11)

I am a House with Four Rooms. I will open and air out each room as a caring and loving gift for myself. (Choices for each are found on p. 13)

Physical_____

Intellectual_____

Emotional _____

Spiritual_____

☾Evening time pondering

What can I look forward to tomorrow?_____

5 things I am thankful for today_____

_____

_____

Sleep revitalizes me. I will prepare for sleep by_____
((Choices for preparation of sleep are on p. 17)

It is in Community that we come to see God in the other. It is in Community that we see our own emptiness filled up. -Sister Joan D. Chittister

Which like-minded people can you be open to? What small groups would you like to be a part of? What age group: children, teens, college kids, older adults, calls to you?

_____

_____

_____

_____

_____

_____

_____

_____

_____

_____

The Power of Self Care/Self Love: A Journal Workbook Into Your Higher Self

The very best thing you can do for the whole world is to make the most of yourself. -Seth Godin

Today is ___/___/___

In this moment I feel_____

I affirm that I am_____
(Choices of affirmations are on p. 9)

Where can I create joy today?_____
(Choices of joys are on p.11)

I am a House with Four Rooms. I will open and air out each room as a caring and loving gift for myself. (Choices for each are found on p. 13)

Physical_____

Intellectual_____

Emotional _____

Spiritual_____

🌙Evening time pondering

What can I look forward to tomorrow?_____

5 things I am thankful for today_____

_____

_____

Sleep revitalizes me. I will prepare for sleep by_____
((Choices for preparation of sleep are on p. 17)

The Power of Self Care/Self Love: A Journal Workbook Into Your Higher Self

Live your life as you see fit. That is not selfish. Selfish is to demand that others live their lives as you see fit.
-Anthony de Mello

Today is ___/___/___

In this moment I feel_____

I affirm that I am_____
(Choices of affirmations are on p. 9)

Where can I create joy today?_____
(Choices of joys are on p.11)

I am a House with Four Rooms. I will open and air out each room as a caring and loving gift for myself. (Choices for each are found on p. 13)

Physical_____

Intellectual_____

Emotional_____

Spiritual_____

🌙Evening time pondering

What can I look forward to tomorrow?_____

5 things I am thankful for today_____

_____

_____

Sleep revitalizes me. I will prepare for sleep by_____
((Choices for preparation of sleep are on p. 17)

I always wanted to be someone better the next day than I was the day before. -Sidney Poitier

Today is ___/___/___

In this moment I feel_____

I affirm that I am_____
(Choices of affirmations are on p. 9)

Where can I create joy today?_____
(Choices of joys are on p.11)

I am a House with Four Rooms. I will open and air out each room as a caring and loving gift for myself. (Choices for each are found on p. 13)

Physical_____

Intellectual_____

Emotional _____

Spiritual_____

☾Evening time pondering

What can I look forward to tomorrow?_____

5 things I am thankful for today_____

_____

_____

Sleep revitalizes me. I will prepare for sleep by_____
((Choices for preparation of sleep are on p. 17)

You cannot live your life looking at yourself from someone else's point of view. -Penelope Cruz

Today is ___/___/___

In this moment I feel_____

I affirm that I am_____
(Choices of affirmations are on p. 9)

Where can I create joy today?_____
(Choices of joys are on p.11)

I am a House with Four Rooms. I will open and air out each room as a caring and loving gift for myself. (Choices for each are found on p. 13)

Physical_____

Intellectual_____

Emotional _____

Spiritual_____

🌙Evening time pondering

What can I look forward to tomorrow?_____

5 things I am thankful for today_____

_____

_____

Sleep revitalizes me. I will prepare for sleep by_____
((Choices for preparation of sleep are on p. 17)

The Power of Self Care/Self Love: A Journal Workbook Into Your Higher Self

There is a crack in everything. That is how the light gets in.
-Leonard Cohen

Today is ___/___/___

In this moment I feel_____

I affirm that I am_____
(Choices of affirmations are on p. 9)

Where can I create joy today?_____
(Choices of joys are on p.11)

I am a House with Four Rooms. I will open and air out each room as a caring and loving gift for myself. (Choices for each are found on p. 13)

Physical_____

Intellectual_____

Emotional _____

Spiritual_____

☾Evening time pondering

What can I look forward to tomorrow?_____

5 things I am thankful for today_____
_____
_____

Sleep revitalizes me. I will prepare for sleep by_____
((Choices for preparation of sleep are on p. 17)

The Power of Self Care/Self Love: A Journal Workbook Into Your Higher Self

If someone ever says you are weird, say thank you.
-Ellen DeGeneres

Today is ___/___/___

In this moment I feel_____

I affirm that I am_____
(Choices of affirmations are on p. 9)

Where can I create joy today?_____
(Choices of joys are on p.11)

I am a House with Four Rooms. I will open and air out each room as a caring and loving gift for myself. (Choices for each are found on p. 13)

Physical_____

Intellectual_____

Emotional _____

Spiritual_____

🌙 Evening time pondering

What can I look forward to tomorrow?_____

5 things I am thankful for today_____

_____

_____

Sleep revitalizes me. I will prepare for sleep by_____
((Choices for preparation of sleep are on p. 17)

In the end some of your greatest pains become your greatest strengths. -Drew Barrymore

On this page if you can, write down the challenging times in your life. Are you a better or stronger person because of them?

_____

_____

_____

_____

_____

_____

_____

_____

_____

_____

_____

_____

_____

_____

The Power of Self Care/Self Love: A Journal Workbook Into Your Higher Self

Do not think of yourself as a small, compressed, suffering thing. Think of yourself as graceful and expanding, no matter how unlikely it may seem at the time. -B.K.S Iyengar

Today is ___/___/___

In this moment I feel_____

I affirm that I am_____
(Choices of affirmations are on p. 9)

Where can I create joy today?_____
(Choices of joys are on p.11)

I am a House with Four Rooms. I will open and air out each room as a caring and loving gift for myself. (Choices for each are found on p. 13)

Physical_____

Intellectual_____

Emotional _____

Spiritual_____

☾Evening time pondering

What can I look forward to tomorrow?_____

5 things I am thankful for today_____

_____

_____

Sleep revitalizes me. I will prepare for sleep by_____
((Choices for preparation of sleep are on p. 17)

What Do You Need?

The Power of Self Care/Self Love: A Journal Workbook Into Your Higher Self

Laughter is an instant vacation. -Milton Berle

Today is ___/___/___

In this moment I feel_____

I affirm that I am_____
(Choices of affirmations are on p. 9)

Where can I create joy today?_____
(Choices of joys are on p.11)

I am a House with Four Rooms. I will open and air out each room as a caring and loving gift for myself. (Choices for each are found on p. 13)

Physical_____

Intellectual_____

Emotional _____

Spiritual_____

☽Evening time pondering

What can I look forward to tomorrow?_____

5 things I am thankful for today_____

_____

_____

Sleep revitalizes me. I will prepare for sleep by_____
((Choices for preparation of sleep are on p. 17)

The Power of Self Care/Self Love: A Journal Workbook Into Your Higher Self

I see the big picture first, then I go backwards to execute it.
-Billie Jean King

Today is ___/___/___

In this moment I feel_____

I affirm that I am_____
(Choices of affirmations are on p. 9)

Where can I create joy today?_____
(Choices of joys are on p.11)

I am a House with Four Rooms. I will open and air out each room as a caring and loving gift for myself. (Choices for each are found on p. 13)

Physical_____

Intellectual_____

Emotional _____

Spiritual_____

🌙Evening time pondering

What can I look forward to tomorrow?_____

5 things I am thankful for today_____

_____

_____

Sleep revitalizes me. I will prepare for sleep by_____
((Choices for preparation of sleep are on p. 17)

The Power of Self Care/Self Love: A Journal Workbook Into Your Higher Self

All is well and you are one with God.

Today is ___/___/___

In this moment I feel_____

I affirm that I am_____
(Choices of affirmations are on p. 9)

Where can I create joy today?_____
(Choices of joys are on p.11)

I am a House with Four Rooms. I will open and air out each room as a caring and loving gift for myself. (Choices for each are found on p. 13)

Physical_____

Intellectual_____

Emotional _____

Spiritual_____

☾Evening time pondering

What can I look forward to tomorrow?_____

5 things I am thankful for today_____

_____

_____

Sleep revitalizes me. I will prepare for sleep by_____
((Choices for preparation of sleep are on p. 17)

What we do and say and show really matters.
-Christiane Amanpour

Today is ___/___/___

In this moment I feel_____

I affirm that I am_____
(Choices of affirmations are on p. 9)

Where can I create joy today?_____
(Choices of joys are on p.11)

I am a House with Four Rooms. I will open and air out each room as a caring and loving gift for myself. (Choices for each are found on p. 13)

Physical_____

Intellectual_____

Emotional _____

Spiritual_____

☾Evening time pondering

What can I look forward to tomorrow?_____

5 things I am thankful for today_____

_____

_____

Sleep revitalizes me. I will prepare for sleep by_____
((Choices for preparation of sleep are on p. 17)

Self-Trust is the first secret of success.
-Ralph Waldo Emerson

Do you trust that you are on the right path?
Write down what your life would be like if you trusted yourself.

_____

_____

_____

_____

_____

_____

_____

_____

_____

_____

_____

_____

_____

The Power of Self Care/Self Love: A Journal Workbook Into Your Higher Self

Acknowledging the good that you already have in your life is the foundation for all abundance. -Eckhart Tolle

Today is ___/___/___

In this moment I feel_____

I affirm that I am_____
(Choices of affirmations are on p. 9)

Where can I create joy today?_____
(Choices of joys are on p.11)

I am a House with Four Rooms. I will open and air out each room as a caring and loving gift for myself. (Choices for each are found on p. 13)

Physical_____

Intellectual_____

Emotional _____

Spiritual_____

♪Evening time pondering

What can I look forward to tomorrow?_____

5 things I am thankful for today_____
_____
_____

Sleep revitalizes me. I will prepare for sleep by_____
((Choices for preparation of sleep are on p. 17)

Never be too busy to listen to your instinctive feelings when something feels wrong. -Marie Osmond

Today is ___/___/___

In this moment I feel_____

I affirm that I am_____
(Choices of affirmations are on p. 9)

Where can I create joy today?_____
(Choices of joys are on p.11)

I am a House with Four Rooms. I will open and air out each room as a caring and loving gift for myself. (Choices for each are found on p. 13)

Physical_____

Intellectual_____

Emotional _____

Spiritual_____

🌙Evening time pondering

What can I look forward to tomorrow?_____

5 things I am thankful for today_____

_____

_____

Sleep revitalizes me. I will prepare for sleep by_____
((Choices for preparation of sleep are on p. 17)

The Power of Self Care/Self Love: A Journal Workbook Into Your Higher Self

No matter how many mistakes you make, or how slow your progress, you are still way ahead of everyone who isn't trying.
-Tony Robbins

Today is ___/___/___

In this moment I feel_____

I affirm that I am_____
(Choices of affirmations are on p. 9)

Where can I create joy today?_____
(Choices of joys are on p.11)

I am a House with Four Rooms. I will open and air out each room as a caring and loving gift for myself. (Choices for each are found on p. 13)

Physical_____

Intellectual_____

Emotional _____

Spiritual_____

☾Evening time pondering

What can I look forward to tomorrow?_____

5 things I am thankful for today_____

_____

_____

Sleep revitalizes me. I will prepare for sleep by_____
((Choices for preparation of sleep are on p. 17)

The Power of Self Care/Self Love: A Journal Workbook Into Your Higher Self

Rise to your higher self.

Today is ___/___/___

In this moment I feel_____

I affirm that I am_____
(Choices of affirmations are on p. 9)

Where can I create joy today?_____
(Choices of joys are on p.11)

I am a House with Four Rooms. I will open and air out each room as a caring and loving gift for myself. (Choices for each are found on p. 13)

Physical_____

Intellectual_____

Emotional _____

Spiritual_____

☾ Evening time pondering

What can I look forward to tomorrow?_____

5 things I am thankful for today_____

_____

_____

Sleep revitalizes me. I will prepare for sleep by_____
((Choices for preparation of sleep are on p. 17)

The Power of Self Care/Self Love: A Journal Workbook Into Your Higher Self

Remember tomorrow is promised to no one. -Walter Payton

Today is ___/___/___

In this moment I feel_____

I affirm that I am_____
(Choices of affirmations are on p. 9)

Where can I create joy today?_____
(Choices of joys are on p.11)

I am a House with Four Rooms. I will open and air out each room as a caring and loving gift for myself. (Choices for each are found on p. 13)

Physical_____

Intellectual_____

Emotional _____

Spiritual_____

☽Evening time pondering

What can I look forward to tomorrow?_____

5 things I am thankful for today_____
_____
_____

Sleep revitalizes me. I will prepare for sleep by_____
((Choices for preparation of sleep are on p. 17)

I do not run away from a challenge because I am afraid. Instead, I run toward it because the only way to escape fear is to trample it beneath your feet. -Nadia Comaneci

Today is ___/___/___

In this moment I feel_____

I affirm that I am_____
(Choices of affirmations are on p. 9)

Where can I create joy today?_____
(Choices of joys are on p.11)

I am a House with Four Rooms. I will open and air out each room as a caring and loving gift for myself. (Choices for each are found on p. 13)

Physical_____

Intellectual_____

Emotional _____

Spiritual_____

🌙Evening time pondering

What can I look forward to tomorrow?_____

5 things I am thankful for today_____

_____

_____

Sleep revitalizes me. I will prepare for sleep by_____
((Choices for preparation of sleep are on p. 17)

Today, pour love into your heart.

Take 5-10 slow, deep breaths. Allow your body to be surrounded by light. Open your heart to this infinite divine loving light. Pour this infinite divine light into your expanding heart. Write down what you feel.

The Power of Self Care/Self Love: A Journal Workbook Into Your Higher Self

Whatever is bringing you down-get rid of it. Because you will find that when you are free, your true creativity, your true self comes out. -Tina Turner

Today is ___/___/___

In this moment I feel_____

I affirm that I am_____
(Choices of affirmations are on p. 9)

Where can I create joy today?_____
(Choices of joys are on p.11)

I am a House with Four Rooms. I will open and air out each room as a caring and loving gift for myself. (Choices for each are found on p. 13)

Physical_____

Intellectual_____

Emotional _____

Spiritual_____

☽Evening time pondering

What can I look forward to tomorrow?_____

5 things I am thankful for today_____

_____

_____

Sleep revitalizes me. I will prepare for sleep by_____
((Choices for preparation of sleep are on p. 17)

The Power of Self Care/Self Love: A Journal Workbook Into Your Higher Self

A life is not significant except for its impact on others' lives.
-Jackie Robinson

Today is ___/___/___

In this moment I feel_____

I affirm that I am_____
(Choices of affirmations are on p. 9)

Where can I create joy today?_____
(Choices of joys are on p.11)

I am a House with Four Rooms. I will open and air out each room as a caring and loving gift for myself. (Choices for each are found on p. 13)

Physical_____

Intellectual_____

Emotional _____

Spiritual_____

☾Evening time pondering

What can I look forward to tomorrow?_____

5 things I am thankful for today_____

_____

_____

Sleep revitalizes me. I will prepare for sleep by_____
((Choices for preparation of sleep are on p. 17)

What Do You Need?

The Power of Self Care/Self Love: A Journal Workbook Into Your Higher Self

The one thing you can give and end up with more is the energy from a hug. -Little Tree/Cherokee Creek

Today is ___/___/___

In this moment I feel_____

I affirm that I am_____
(Choices of affirmations are on p. 9)

Where can I create joy today?_____
(Choices of joys are on p.11)

I am a House with Four Rooms. I will open and air out each room as a caring and loving gift for myself. (Choices for each are found on p. 13)

Physical_____

Intellectual_____

Emotional _____

Spiritual_____

☾Evening time pondering

What can I look forward to tomorrow?_____

5 things I am thankful for today_____

_____

_____

Sleep revitalizes me. I will prepare for sleep by_____
((Choices for preparation of sleep are on p. 17)

The Power of Self Care/Self Love: A Journal Workbook Into Your Higher Self

A journey of a thousand miles must begin with a single step.
-Lao Tzu

Today is ___/___/___

In this moment I feel_____

I affirm that I am_____
(Choices of affirmations are on p. 9)

Where can I create joy today?_____
(Choices of joys are on p.11)

I am a House with Four Rooms. I will open and air out each room as a caring and loving gift for myself. (Choices for each are found on p. 13)

Physical_____

Intellectual_____

Emotional _____

Spiritual_____

☾Evening time pondering

What can I look forward to tomorrow?_____

5 things I am thankful for today_____

_____

_____

Sleep revitalizes me. I will prepare for sleep by_____
((Choices for preparation of sleep are on p. 17)

A friend is someone with whom you dare to be yourself.
-Frank Crane

Today is ___/___/___

In this moment I feel_____

I affirm that I am_____
(Choices of affirmations are on p. 9)

Where can I create joy today?_____
(Choices of joys are on p.11)

I am a House with Four Rooms. I will open and air out each room as a caring and loving gift for myself. (Choices for each are found on p. 13)

Physical_____

Intellectual_____

Emotional _____

Spiritual_____

☽Evening time pondering

What can I look forward to tomorrow?_____

5 things I am thankful for today_____

_____

_____

Sleep revitalizes me. I will prepare for sleep by_____
((Choices for preparation of sleep are on p. 17)

The Power of Self Care/Self Love: A Journal Workbook Into Your Higher Self

Nothing is impossible. The word itself says, "I'm possible"! -Audrey Hepburn

When your mind says, "No I can't do that" what does that feel like in your body? When your mind says, "Maybe I can do that" what does that feel like in your body?

_____
_____
_____
_____
_____
_____
_____
_____
_____
_____
_____
_____
_____
_____

The Power of Self Care/Self Love: A Journal Workbook Into Your Higher Self

The simple things are also the most extraordinary things, and only the wise can see them. -Paulo Coelho

Today is ___/___/___

In this moment I feel_____

I affirm that I am_____
(Choices of affirmations are on p. 9)

Where can I create joy today?_____
(Choices of joys are on p.11)

I am a House with Four Rooms. I will open and air out each room as a caring and loving gift for myself. (Choices for each are found on p. 13)

Physical_____

Intellectual_____

Emotional _____

Spiritual_____

☾Evening time pondering

What can I look forward to tomorrow?_____

5 things I am thankful for today_____

_____

_____

Sleep revitalizes me. I will prepare for sleep by_____
((Choices for preparation of sleep are on p. 17)

The Power of Self Care/Self Love: A Journal Workbook Into Your Higher Self

Yesterday I was clever, so I wanted to change the world. Today I am wise, so I am changing myself. -Rumi

Today is ___/___/___

In this moment I feel_____

I affirm that I am_____
(Choices of affirmations are on p. 9)

Where can I create joy today?_____
(Choices of joys are on p.11)

I am a House with Four Rooms. I will open and air out each room as a caring and loving gift for myself. (Choices for each are found on p. 13)

Physical_____

Intellectual_____

Emotional _____

Spiritual_____

☾Evening time pondering

What can I look forward to tomorrow?_____

5 things I am thankful for today_____

_____

_____

Sleep revitalizes me. I will prepare for sleep by_____
((Choices for preparation of sleep are on p. 17)

The Power of Self Care/Self Love: A Journal Workbook Into Your Higher Self

Learn to light a candle in the darkest moments of someone's life. Be the light that helps others see; it is what gives life its deepest significance. -Roy T. Bennett

Today is ___/___/___

In this moment I feel_____

I affirm that I am_____
(Choices of affirmations are on p. 9)

Where can I create joy today?_____
(Choices of joys are on p.11)

I am a House with Four Rooms. I will open and air out each room as a caring and loving gift for myself. (Choices for each are found on p. 13)

Physical_____

Intellectual_____

Emotional _____

Spiritual_____

🌙Evening time pondering

What can I look forward to tomorrow?_____

5 things I am thankful for today_____

_____

_____

Sleep revitalizes me. I will prepare for sleep by_____
((Choices for preparation of sleep are on p. 17)

The Power of Self Care/Self Love: A Journal Workbook Into Your Higher Self

And God said, love your enemy, & I obeyed Him & loved myself.
-Khalil Gibran

Today is ___/___/___

In this moment I feel_____

I affirm that I am_____
(Choices of affirmations are on p. 9)

Where can I create joy today?_____
(Choices of joys are on p.11)

I am a House with Four Rooms. I will open and air out each room as a caring and loving gift for myself. (Choices for each are found on p. 13)

Physical_____

Intellectual_____

Emotional _____

Spiritual_____

☾Evening time pondering

What can I look forward to tomorrow?_____

5 things I am thankful for today_____
_____
_____

Sleep revitalizes me. I will prepare for sleep by_____
((Choices for preparation of sleep are on p. 17)

The Power of Self Care/Self Love: A Journal Workbook Into Your Higher Self

If you want to see the true measure of a man, watch how he treats his inferiors, not his equals. -J.K. Rowling

Today is ___/___/___

In this moment I feel_____

I affirm that I am_____
(Choices of affirmations are on p. 9)

Where can I create joy today?_____
(Choices of joys are on p.11)

I am a House with Four Rooms. I will open and air out each room as a caring and loving gift for myself. (Choices for each are found on p. 13)

Physical_____

Intellectual_____

Emotional_____

Spiritual_____

🌙Evening time pondering

What can I look forward to tomorrow?_____

5 things I am thankful for today_____

_____

_____

Sleep revitalizes me. I will prepare for sleep by_____
((Choices for preparation of sleep are on p. 17)

The Power of Self Care/Self Love: A Journal Workbook Into Your Higher Self

Eventually, you will come to understand that love heals everything, and love is all there is. -Gary Zukav

Today is ___/___/___

In this moment I feel_____

I affirm that I am_____
(Choices of affirmations are on p. 9)

Where can I create joy today?_____
(Choices of joys are on p.11)

I am a House with Four Rooms. I will open and air out each room as a caring and loving gift for myself. (Choices for each are found on p. 13)

Physical_____

Intellectual_____

Emotional _____

Spiritual_____

🌙Evening time pondering

What can I look forward to tomorrow?_____

5 things I am thankful for today_____

_____

_____

Sleep revitalizes me. I will prepare for sleep by_____
((Choices for preparation of sleep are on p. 17)

To acquire knowledge, one must study; but to acquire wisdom, one must observe. -Marilyn Vos Savant

Your home, big or small, is a place of refuge. Take a few minutes today and walk into each room as you observe how you feel. Write down one simple change you can make that will create loving comfort.

The Power of Self Care/Self Love: A Journal Workbook Into Your Higher Self

Knowledge speaks, but wisdom listens. -Jimi Hendrix

Today is ___/___/___

In this moment I feel_____

I affirm that I am_____
(Choices of affirmations are on p. 9)

Where can I create joy today?_____
(Choices of joys are on p.11)

I am a House with Four Rooms. I will open and air out each room as a caring and loving gift for myself. (Choices for each are found on p. 13)

Physical_____

Intellectual_____

Emotional _____

Spiritual_____

🌙Evening time pondering

What can I look forward to tomorrow?_____

5 things I am thankful for today_____

_____

_____

Sleep revitalizes me. I will prepare for sleep by_____
((Choices for preparation of sleep are on p. 17)

The Power of Self Care/Self Love: A Journal Workbook Into Your Higher Self

Rather fail with honor than succeed by fraud. -Sophocles

Today is ___/___/___

In this moment I feel_____

I affirm that I am_____
(Choices of affirmations are on p. 9)

Where can I create joy today?_____
(Choices of joys are on p.11)

I am a House with Four Rooms. I will open and air out each room as a caring and loving gift for myself. (Choices for each are found on p. 13)

Physical_____

Intellectual_____

Emotional _____

Spiritual_____

🌙Evening time pondering

What can I look forward to tomorrow?_____

5 things I am thankful for today_____

_____

_____

Sleep revitalizes me. I will prepare for sleep by_____
((Choices for preparation of sleep are on p. 17)

What Do You Need?

The Power of Self Care/Self Love: A Journal Workbook Into Your Higher Self

The vibrations on the air are the breath of God speaking to man's soul. -Ludwig van Beethoven

Today is ___/___/___

In this moment I feel_____

I affirm that I am_____
(Choices of affirmations are on p. 9)

Where can I create joy today?_____
(Choices of joys are on p.11)

I am a House with Four Rooms. I will open and air out each room as a caring and loving gift for myself. (Choices for each are found on p. 13)

Physical_____

Intellectual_____

Emotional _____

Spiritual_____

☾Evening time pondering

What can I look forward to tomorrow?_____

5 things I am thankful for today_____

_____

_____

Sleep revitalizes me. I will prepare for sleep by_____
((Choices for preparation of sleep are on p. 17)

The Power of Self Care/Self Love: A Journal Workbook Into Your Higher Self

The desire to reach for the stars is ambitious. The desire to reach hearts is wise. -Maya Angelou

Today is ___/___/___

In this moment I feel_____

I affirm that I am_____
(Choices of affirmations are on p. 9)

Where can I create joy today?_____
(Choices of joys are on p.11)

I am a House with Four Rooms. I will open and air out each room as a caring and loving gift for myself. (Choices for each are found on p. 13)

Physical_____

Intellectual_____

Emotional _____

Spiritual_____

♪Evening time pondering

What can I look forward to tomorrow?_____

5 things I am thankful for today_____

_____

_____

Sleep revitalizes me. I will prepare for sleep by_____
((Choices for preparation of sleep are on p. 17)

The Power of Self Care/Self Love: A Journal Workbook Into Your Higher Self

Love One Another. -Jesus

Today is ___/___/___

In this moment I feel_____

I affirm that I am_____
(Choices of affirmations are on p. 9)

Where can I create joy today?_____
(Choices of joys are on p.11)

I am a House with Four Rooms. I will open and air out each room as a caring and loving gift for myself. (Choices for each are found on p. 13)

Physical_____

Intellectual_____

Emotional _____

Spiritual_____

🌙Evening time pondering

What can I look forward to tomorrow?_____

5 things I am thankful for today_____

_____

_____

Sleep revitalizes me. I will prepare for sleep by_____
((Choices for preparation of sleep are on p. 17)

Whatever you believe, you will find that you are correct. The universe has a way of presenting...exactly what you believe. If you think life is great, you are correct. If you think life is tough, you will be proved correct too.
−Anita Moorjani

Fill this page with your new beliefs.

_____

_____

_____

_____

_____

_____

_____

_____

_____

_____

_____

The Power of Self Care/Self Love: A Journal Workbook Into Your Higher Self

I realized that my battle to survive this war would have to be fought inside of me. -Immaculee Ilibagiza

Today is ___/___/___

In this moment I feel_____

I affirm that I am_____
(Choices of affirmations are on p. 9)

Where can I create joy today?_____
(Choices of joys are on p.11)

I am a House with Four Rooms. I will open and air out each room as a caring and loving gift for myself. (Choices for each are found on p. 13)

Physical_____

Intellectual_____

Emotional _____

Spiritual_____

☾Evening time pondering

What can I look forward to tomorrow?_____

5 things I am thankful for today_____

_____

_____

Sleep revitalizes me. I will prepare for sleep by_____
((Choices for preparation of sleep are on p. 17)

The Power of Self Care/Self Love: A Journal Workbook Into Your Higher Self

If you think that you are too small to make a difference, try sleeping with a mosquito. -Dalai Lama

Today is ___/___/___

In this moment I feel_____

I affirm that I am_____
(Choices of affirmations are on p. 9)

Where can I create joy today?_____
(Choices of joys are on p.11)

I am a House with Four Rooms. I will open and air out each room as a caring and loving gift for myself. (Choices for each are found on p. 13)

Physical_____

Intellectual_____

Emotional_____

Spiritual_____

🌙Evening time pondering

What can I look forward to tomorrow?_____

5 things I am thankful for today_____
_____
_____

Sleep revitalizes me. I will prepare for sleep by_____
((Choices for preparation of sleep are on p. 17)

Life is full of surprises and serendipity. Being open to unexpected turns in the road is an important part of success.
-Condoleeza Rice

Today is ___/___/___

In this moment I feel_____

I affirm that I am_____
(Choices of affirmations are on p. 9)

Where can I create joy today?_____
(Choices of joys are on p.11)

I am a House with Four Rooms. I will open and air out each room as a caring and loving gift for myself. (Choices for each are found on p. 13)

Physical_____

Intellectual_____

Emotional _____

Spiritual_____

🌙 Evening time pondering

What can I look forward to tomorrow?_____

5 things I am thankful for today_____

_____

_____

Sleep revitalizes me. I will prepare for sleep by_____
((Choices for preparation of sleep are on p. 17)

The Power of Self Care/Self Love: A Journal Workbook Into Your Higher Self

Hold someone in your arms today.

Today is ___/___/___

In this moment I feel_____

I affirm that I am_____
(Choices of affirmations are on p. 9)

Where can I create joy today?_____
(Choices of joys are on p.11)

I am a House with Four Rooms. I will open and air out each room as a caring and loving gift for myself. (Choices for each are found on p. 13)

Physical_____

Intellectual_____

Emotional _____

Spiritual_____

🌙Evening time pondering

What can I look forward to tomorrow?_____

5 things I am thankful for today_____

_____

_____

Sleep revitalizes me. I will prepare for sleep by_____
((Choices for preparation of sleep are on p. 17)

The Power of Self Care/Self Love: A Journal Workbook Into Your Higher Self

If you do not find peace within, you will not find it anywhere else. The Goal of Life is the attainment of Peace and not the achievement of power, name, fame, and wealth. -Sivananda

Today is ___/___/___

In this moment I feel_____

I affirm that I am_____
(Choices of affirmations are on p. 9)

Where can I create joy today?_____
(Choices of joys are on p.11)

I am a House with Four Rooms. I will open and air out each room as a caring and loving gift for myself. (Choices for each are found on p. 13)

Physical_____

Intellectual_____

Emotional _____

Spiritual_____

☾Evening time pondering

What can I look forward to tomorrow?_____

5 things I am thankful for today_____

_____

_____

Sleep revitalizes me. I will prepare for sleep by_____
((Choices for preparation of sleep are on p. 17)

The Power of Self Care/Self Love: A Journal Workbook Into Your Higher Self

Acceptance is the key to being truly free. -Katy Perry

Today is ___/___/___

In this moment I feel_____

I affirm that I am_____
(Choices of affirmations are on p. 9)

Where can I create joy today?_____
(Choices of joys are on p.11)

I am a House with Four Rooms. I will open and air out each room as a caring and loving gift for myself. (Choices for each are found on p. 13)

Physical_____

Intellectual_____

Emotional _____

Spiritual_____

☾Evening time pondering

What can I look forward to tomorrow?_____

5 things I am thankful for today_____

_____

_____

Sleep revitalizes me. I will prepare for sleep by_____
((Choices for preparation of sleep are on p. 17)

We are losing the way of understanding nature and that processed food doesn't have light. If we are going to eat anything it should be intact. It should have the optimum amount of light, so it is healthy for us to nourish the body and the spirit.
-13th Grandmother Flordemayo

The Gut and Brain Axis shows us the connection between the food we eat, our cognition and emotions. List the foods that you love that grow from the earth. Can you add two of them to each meal or snack?

_____

_____

_____

_____

_____

_____

_____

_____

_____

_____

The Power of Self Care/Self Love: A Journal Workbook Into Your Higher Self

Taste all the flavors in your food today.

Today is ___/___/___

In this moment I feel_____

I affirm that I am_____
(Choices of affirmations are on p. 9)

Where can I create joy today?_____
(Choices of joys are on p.11)

I am a House with Four Rooms. I will open and air out each room as a caring and loving gift for myself. (Choices for each are found on p. 13)

Physical_____

Intellectual_____

Emotional _____

Spiritual_____

🌙Evening time pondering

What can I look forward to tomorrow?_____

5 things I am thankful for today_____

_____

_____

Sleep revitalizes me. I will prepare for sleep by_____
((Choices for preparation of sleep are on p. 17)

The Power of Self Care/Self Love: A Journal Workbook Into Your Higher Self

Half of seeming clever is keeping your mouth shut at the right times. -Patrick Rothfuss

Today is ___/___/___

In this moment I feel_____

I affirm that I am_____
(Choices of affirmations are on p. 9)

Where can I create joy today?_____
(Choices of joys are on p.11)

I am a House with Four Rooms. I will open and air out each room as a caring and loving gift for myself. (Choices for each are found on p. 13)

Physical_____

Intellectual_____

Emotional _____

Spiritual_____

☾Evening time pondering

What can I look forward to tomorrow?_____

5 things I am thankful for today_____

_____

_____

Sleep revitalizes me. I will prepare for sleep by_____
((Choices for preparation of sleep are on p. 17)

The Power of Self Care/Self Love: A Journal Workbook Into Your Higher Self

Life would be tragic if it were not funny. -Stephen Hawking

Today is ___/___/___

In this moment I feel_____

I affirm that I am_____
(Choices of affirmations are on p. 9)

Where can I create joy today?_____
(Choices of joys are on p.11)

I am a House with Four Rooms. I will open and air out each room as a caring and loving gift for myself. (Choices for each are found on p. 13)

Physical_____

Intellectual_____

Emotional _____

Spiritual_____

🌙Evening time pondering

What can I look forward to tomorrow?_____

5 things I am thankful for today_____

_____

_____

Sleep revitalizes me. I will prepare for sleep by_____
((Choices for preparation of sleep are on p. 17)

What Do You Need?

The Power of Self Care/Self Love: A Journal Workbook Into Your Higher Self

Become aware that you already possess all the inner wisdom, strength, and creativity needed to make your dreams come true.
-Sarah Ban Breathnach

Today is ___/___/___

In this moment I feel_____

I affirm that I am_____
(Choices of affirmations are on p. 9)

Where can I create joy today?_____
(Choices of joys are on p.11)

I am a House with Four Rooms. I will open and air out each room as a caring and loving gift for myself. (Choices for each are found on p. 13)

Physical_____

Intellectual_____

Emotional _____

Spiritual_____

☾Evening time pondering

What can I look forward to tomorrow?_____

5 things I am thankful for today_____

_____

_____

Sleep revitalizes me. I will prepare for sleep by_____
((Choices for preparation of sleep are on p. 17)

The Power of Self Care/Self Love: A Journal Workbook Into Your Higher Self

Shift into your own ability to heal.

Today is ___/___/___

In this moment I feel_____

I affirm that I am_____
(Choices of affirmations are on p. 9)

Where can I create joy today?_____
(Choices of joys are on p.11)

I am a House with Four Rooms. I will open and air out each room as a caring and loving gift for myself. (Choices for each are found on p. 13)

Physical_____

Intellectual_____

Emotional _____

Spiritual_____

☾Evening time pondering

What can I look forward to tomorrow?_____

5 things I am thankful for today_____

_____

_____

Sleep revitalizes me. I will prepare for sleep by_____
((Choices for preparation of sleep are on p. 17)

Be kinder to yourself. And then let your kindness flood the world. -Pema Chodron

List the ways you can be kinder to yourself. List the ways you can be kinder to your partner or close friend.

_____

_____

_____

_____

_____

_____

_____

_____

_____

_____

_____

_____

The Power of Self Care/Self Love: A Journal Workbook Into Your Higher Self

There is nothing noble in being superior to some other man. The true nobility is in being superior to your previous self.
-Hindu proverb

Today is ___/___/___

In this moment I feel_____

I affirm that I am_____
(Choices of affirmations are on p. 9)

Where can I create joy today?_____
(Choices of joys are on p.11)

I am a House with Four Rooms. I will open and air out each room as a caring and loving gift for myself. (Choices for each are found on p. 13)

Physical_____

Intellectual_____

Emotional _____

Spiritual_____

☾Evening time pondering

What can I look forward to tomorrow?_____

5 things I am thankful for today_____

_____

_____

Sleep revitalizes me. I will prepare for sleep by_____
((Choices for preparation of sleep are on p. 17)

The Power of Self Care/Self Love: A Journal Workbook Into Your Higher Self

Spread your wings...it is time.

Today is ___/___/___

In this moment I feel_____

I affirm that I am_____
(Choices of affirmations are on p. 9)

Where can I create joy today?_____
(Choices of joys are on p.11)

I am a House with Four Rooms. I will open and air out each room as a caring and loving gift for myself. (Choices for each are found on p. 13)

Physical_____

Intellectual_____

Emotional _____

Spiritual_____

☾Evening time pondering

What can I look forward to tomorrow?_____

5 things I am thankful for today_____

_____

_____

Sleep revitalizes me. I will prepare for sleep by_____
((Choices for preparation of sleep are on p. 17)

The Power of Self Care/Self Love: A Journal Workbook Into Your Higher Self

There is something wonderfully bold and liberating about saying yes to our entire imperfect and messy life. -Tara Brach

Today is ___/___/___

In this moment I feel_____

I affirm that I am_____
(Choices of affirmations are on p. 9)

Where can I create joy today?_____
(Choices of joys are on p.11)

I am a House with Four Rooms. I will open and air out each room as a caring and loving gift for myself. (Choices for each are found on p. 13)

Physical_____

Intellectual_____

Emotional _____

Spiritual_____

☾Evening time pondering

What can I look forward to tomorrow?_____

5 things I am thankful for today_____

_____

_____

Sleep revitalizes me. I will prepare for sleep by_____
((Choices for preparation of sleep are on p. 17)

If I knew that this would be the last time I would hear your voice, I'd take hold of each word to be able to hear it over and over. If I knew this is the last time I see you, I'd tell you I love you, and would not just assume foolishly you know it already. -
Gabriel Garcia Marquez

Today is ___/___/___

In this moment I feel_____

I affirm that I am_____
(Choices of affirmations are on p. 9)

Where can I create joy today?_____
(Choices of joys are on p.11)

I am a House with Four Rooms. I will open and air out each room as a caring and loving gift for myself. (Choices for each are found on p. 13)

Physical_____

Intellectual_____

Emotional _____

Spiritual_____

☾Evening time pondering

What can I look forward to tomorrow?_____

5 things I am thankful for today_____

_____

_____

Sleep revitalizes me. I will prepare for sleep by_____
((Choices for preparation of sleep are on p. 17)

The way the world underestimates me will be my greatest weapon. -Calista Flockhart

Today is ___/___/___

In this moment I feel_____

I affirm that I am_____
(Choices of affirmations are on p. 9)

Where can I create joy today?_____
(Choices of joys are on p.11)

I am a House with Four Rooms. I will open and air out each room as a caring and loving gift for myself. (Choices for each are found on p. 13)

Physical_____

Intellectual_____

Emotional_____

Spiritual_____

☾Evening time pondering

What can I look forward to tomorrow?_____

5 things I am thankful for today_____

_____

_____

Sleep revitalizes me. I will prepare for sleep by_____
((Choices for preparation of sleep are on p. 17)

The Power of Self Care/Self Love: A Journal Workbook Into Your Higher Self

If there is a heaven for me, I'm sure it has a beach attached.
-Jimmy Buffett

Today is ___/___/___

In this moment I feel_____

I affirm that I am_____
(Choices of affirmations are on p. 9)

Where can I create joy today?_____
(Choices of joys are on p.11)

I am a House with Four Rooms. I will open and air out each room as a caring and loving gift for myself. (Choices for each are found on p. 13)

Physical_____

Intellectual_____

Emotional _____

Spiritual_____

☽Evening time pondering

What can I look forward to tomorrow?_____

5 things I am thankful for today_____

_____

_____

Sleep revitalizes me. I will prepare for sleep by_____
((Choices for preparation of sleep are on p. 17)

What do you need to say today?

With kind words on the left side of this page, list the things you need to say to yourself. On the right side list the things you need to say to someone else.

The Power of Self Care/Self Love: A Journal Workbook Into Your Higher Self

I have one life and one chance to make it count for something.
-Jimmy Carter

Today is ___/___/___

In this moment I feel_____

I affirm that I am_____
(Choices of affirmations are on p. 9)

Where can I create joy today?_____
(Choices of joys are on p.11)

I am a House with Four Rooms. I will open and air out each room as a caring and loving gift for myself. (Choices for each are found on p. 13)

Physical_____

Intellectual_____

Emotional _____

Spiritual_____

☾Evening time pondering

What can I look forward to tomorrow?_____

5 things I am thankful for today_____

_____

_____

Sleep revitalizes me. I will prepare for sleep by_____
((Choices for preparation of sleep are on p. 17)

The Power of Self Care/Self Love: A Journal Workbook Into Your Higher Self

In the end just three things matter: How well we have lived, how well we have loved, how well we have learned to let go.
-Jack Kornfield

Today is ___/___/___

In this moment I feel_____

I affirm that I am_____
(Choices of affirmations are on p. 9)

Where can I create joy today?_____
(Choices of joys are on p.11)

I am a House with Four Rooms. I will open and air out each room as a caring and loving gift for myself. (Choices for each are found on p. 13)

Physical_____

Intellectual_____

Emotional _____

Spiritual_____

🌙Evening time pondering

What can I look forward to tomorrow?_____

5 things I am thankful for today_____

_____

_____

Sleep revitalizes me. I will prepare for sleep by_____
((Choices for preparation of sleep are on p. 17)

Vision Board #4
What I Am Grateful For?

It has been 360 days and it's time to indulge yourself with the last vision board, Gratitude.

Most of what we cut out for vision boards is what we need or want. With this last board, I'd love for you to become aware of what you already have. To see an entire board filled with what you already have is incredibly powerful and healing.

Like a scavenger hunt, look for what you have cut out or printed and taped to the last 10 pages. If there is not much there, take some time today to explore magazines, newspapers, Pinterest, or Canva and cut out or print your items on an 11x14 (or larger) cork board, thick poster board, magnetic dry erase board, or canvas.

There are no rules, just a fun exploration of what your body, mind and spirit want to be grateful for.

This Vision board can have:
Handwritten thank you notes.
A love letter/note from someone or from yourself.
A dried flower
sticky notes
Colored paper sheets
3x5 index cards
A poem
Well-thought-out typed words
Pictures of what you are grateful for.
Real pictures of you, family, friends.

Remember, this is a fun activity so grab your scissors, glue, scotch tape, markers, push pins or magnets.

The Power of Self Care/Self Love: A Journal Workbook Into Your Higher Self

The Power of Self Care/Self Love: A Journal Workbook Into Your Higher Self

We shall not cease from exploration, and the end of all our exploring will be to arrive where we started and know the place for the first time. -T.S. Eliot

Today is ___/___/___

In this moment I feel_____

I affirm that I am_____
(Choices of affirmations are on p. 9)

Where can I create joy today?_____
(Choices of joys are on p.11)

I am a House with Four Rooms. I will open and air out each room as a caring and loving gift for myself. (Choices for each are found on p. 13)

Physical_____

Intellectual_____

Emotional_____

Spiritual_____

☾Evening time pondering

What can I look forward to tomorrow?_____

5 things I am thankful for today_____

_____

_____

Sleep revitalizes me. I will prepare for sleep by_____
((Choices for preparation of sleep are on p. 17)

The Power of Self Care/Self Love: A Journal Workbook Into Your Higher Self

Blank page
to collect Vision Board inserts or thoughts

The Power of Self Care/Self Love: A Journal Workbook Into Your Higher Self

Blank page
to collect Vision Board inserts or thoughts

The Power of Self Care/Self Love: A Journal Workbook Into Your Higher Self

Blank page
to collect Vision Board inserts or thoughts

The Power of Self Care/Self Love: A Journal Workbook Into Your Higher Self

Blank page
to collect Vision Board inserts or thoughts

The Power of Self Care/Self Love: A Journal Workbook Into Your Higher Self

Blank page
to collect Vision Board inserts or thoughts

The Power of Self Care/Self Love: A Journal Workbook Into Your Higher Self

Blank page
to collect Vision Board inserts or thoughts

The Power of Self Care/Self Love: A Journal Workbook Into Your Higher Self

Blank page
to collect Vision Board inserts or thoughts

Blank page
to collect Vision Board inserts or thoughts

The Power of Self Care/Self Love: A Journal Workbook Into Your Higher Self

Blank page
to collect Vision Board inserts or thoughts

The Power of Self Care/Self Love: A Journal Workbook Into Your Higher Self

Blank page
to collect Vision Board inserts or thoughts

Everything is Infinite

The purpose of creating The power of Self Care/Self Love journal workbook was to connect you with yourself/God/Universe every day. Each quote was chosen to uplift and support you and keep you in a state of high vibrational frequency of infinite love and light.

This journal is a tool to inspire more care and love for yourself through the exploratory questions: In this moment what are you feeling? What do you affirm? Where can you create joy today? What will you choose to do physically, intellectually, emotionally, and spiritually? And in the evening, what can you look forward to tomorrow? What are the 5 things that happened today for which you are thankful? And how can you prepare for the revitalizing time of sleep?

The vision boards were to bring you closer to what matters to you, clear the path for manifestation, and to awaken your creativity. I recommend that you display them in your bedroom, office, or bathroom so they can inspire you every day.

We have included mandalas to provide a sacred space to aid in meditation as you colored them in, one section at a time. Feel free to take them out and frame them. You can place them on a shelf or corner table to create an actual meditative sacred space.

This journal is now the safe keeper of your evolutionary metamorphosis. You are now the butterfly because you poured your heart out each day as you shed your old self to spread your wings and fly!

Congratulations!

Now find another beautiful journal to keep up the momentum or buy this one again to continue onto your next evolution. This is only the beginning!

With love and health (Con amor y salud),

Jackie Castro-Cooper, MPT

In Gratitude

Thank you to my husband, Scott, who supported me and kept me fed and going during the creation of this loving journal. I would like to thank my editor, Nicole Langton, for sticking with me till the end and moving me in the right direction. To my publisher, John O'Melveny Woods, at Intellect Publishing, who believes in me and goes the extra mile-and sometimes 10,000 miles.

Thank you Betty Sue O'Brian and Dr. Casey Maugh Funderburk for a global edit with wonderful comments and direction. Thank you to Ms. Melz for the creation of the beautiful Mandalas, and thank you to Michael for the wonderful cover design.

And thank you to YOU, the journaler and voyager. I pray that this has been the conduit to your higher self.

Jackie Castro-Cooper

The Power of Self Care/Self Love: A Journal Workbook Into Your Higher Self

Endnotes

#1. https://numerologist.com/numerology/meaning-mystery-and-magic-of-the-number-7/

#2. https://angelnumber.org/15-angel-number-meaning-and-symbolism/

#3. https://www.ridingthebeast.com/numbers/nu40.php

#4. https://www.ridingthebeast.com/numbers/nu90.php

About the Author

Jackie is one of the first holistic, alternative physical therapists in the US. She obtained her Master's in physical therapy from the University of South Alabama. She is a professional speaker, health and business consultant, and the author of, *The Power of Self Care/Self Love: A Physical Therapist's Guide to Evolving Into Your Higher Self* with Intellect Publishing. Her virtual one-hour treatments combine all that she has learned in the past 16 years to take you from pain to true healing.

In 2020 when she couldn't personally treat some of her patients, she created an online self-treatment video series. This allowed people to relieve their physical, emotional, and spiritual pain in their own homes and now all over the world: *Back and Neck Pain Relief: The Surprising Gut and Brain Connection*, available at you-can-heal.teachable.com

Her mission in life is to share information that is not widely known specifically for the alleviation of pain and suffering. Jackie is also the creator of the "Women's Health Forum" which educates and promotes alternative health care for our communities. She also leads, The Self Care/Self Love Retreats.

Her private practice was born in 2007, Gulf Coast Myofascial Release Physical Therapy. She specializes in John F Barnes MFR and incorporates her other studies to fit the needs of her clients. Jackie supports those seeking to combine both evidence-based research and spiritual healing practices.

Jackie is a long-time board member of STEPS Coalition focused on the needs of the underserved. She is a volunteer for CureMSD, a nonprofit that is seeking to eradicate this disease that takes the lives of children before the age of ten. A volunteer for MS Heroes, a nonprofit that uplifts and supports Caregivers. She is also the founder of, The Alliance for the Education of Undocumented Youth that supports DREAMERS.

She ca be seen in Gulf Coast Woman Magazine, WLOX, the Dr. Liana Show, and the February 2021 cover of Success Women's Magazine.

You can receive her monthly E-newsletter with self-treatment video's that she only shares with her subscribers by subscribing on her website gcmfr.com.

Made in United States
Orlando, FL
23 March 2022